WORK
Reimagined

Uncover Your Calling

WORK
Reimagined

Richard J. Leider

David A. Shapiro

Foreword by
Jo Ann Jenkins, CEO, AARP

BK Berrett–Koehler Publishers, Inc.
San Francisco, *www.bk–life.com*

LifeReimagined.org
Real Possibilities from **AARP**

Berrett-Koehler Publishers, Inc.
1333 Broadway, Suite 1000
Oakland, CA 94612-1921
Tel: (510) 817-2277   Fax: (510) 817-2278   www.bkconnection.com

Ordering Information

Quantity sales. Special discounts are available on quantity purchases by corporations, associations, and others. For details, contact the "Special Sales Department" at the Berrett-Koehler address above.

Individual sales. Berrett-Koehler publications are available through most bookstores. They can also be ordered directly from Berrett-Koehler: Tel: (800) 929-2929; Fax: (802) 864-7626; www.bkconnection.com

Orders for college textbook/course adoption use. Please contact Berrett-Koehler: Tel: (800) 929-2929; Fax: (802) 864-7626.

Orders by U.S. trade bookstores and wholesalers. Please contact Ingram Publisher Services, Tel: (800) 509-4887; Fax: (800) 838-1149; E-mail: customer.service@ingrampublisherservices.com; or visit www.ingrampublisherservices.com/Ordering for details about electronic ordering.

Berrett-Koehler and the BK logo are registered trademarks of Berrett-Koehler Publishers, Inc.

Portions of this book have been adapted and revised from Whistle While You Work, Leider and Shapiro, 2001.

AARP and Life Reimagined are registered trademarks of AARP. All rights reserved.

Printed in the United States of America

Berrett-Koehler books are printed on long-lasting acid-free paper. When it is available, we choose paper that has been manufactured by environmentally responsible processes. These may include using trees grown in sustainable forests, incorporating recycled paper, minimizing chlorine in bleaching, or recycling the energy produced at the paper mill.

Library of Congress Cataloging-in-Publication Data

Leider, Richard, author.
Work reimagined : uncover your calling / Richard J. Leider, David A. Shapiro ; foreword by Jo Ann Jenkins. -- First edition.
     pages cm
ISBN 978-1-62656-558-6 (pbk.)
1. Vocational guidance. 2. Vocation. 3. Job satisfaction. 4. Career changes. I. Shapiro, David A., 1957- author. II. Title.
HF5381.L35153 2015
650.1--dc23
                          2015027719
First Edition

20 19 18 17 16 15   10 9 8 7 6 5 4 3 2 1

Cover Designer: Dan Tesser, Studio Carnelian
Text Designer: Lisa Devenish, Devenish Design
Copyeditor: Susan Schmid, Teton Editorial

DEDICATION

*To all those who have uncovered their calling
to find a living worth living.*

CONTENTS

Foreword by Jo Ann Jenkins • ix

PREFACE

Reimagined Lives • xi

INTRODUCTION

The End of Work As We Know It • 1

CHAPTER 1

Reimagining Work—What Do You Do? • 21

CHAPTER 2

Reimagining Calling—Should You Quit Your Day Job? • 45

CHAPTER 3

Reimagining Gifts—How Do You Do It? • 73

CHAPTER 4

Reimagining Passions—Why Do You Do It? • 93

CHAPTER 5

Reimagining Values—Where Do You Do It? • 111

CHAPTER 6

Reimagining Legacy—Have You Played Your Music? • 127

Resources • 149

Index • 151

About the Authors • 157

FOREWORD

....

When Richard Leider asked me to write the foreword to this important new book, *Work Reimagined: Uncovering Your Calling*, it immediately struck me how his request perfectly illustrates a number of the ways in which our world is radically changing.

As the Chief Executive Officer of AARP, an organization of nearly thirty-eight million people 50-plus, I see firsthand how rapidly and dramatically the world of work is changing. It is no longer what it once was, even as recently as a decade ago. More and more of our members want to keep working past traditional retirement age because they want to continue to contribute to society and find meaning in their own lives, and work does that for them.

But, that is having a disruptive influence on the workplace because it goes against old norms and stereotypes. As individuals, and in our organizations, we need to get to the point where we are no longer defined by the old expectations of what we should do or should not do at a certain age, and that means we need to reimagine our lives so we can be open to joy and fulfillment throughout our days. After all, it is not really about aging; it is about living.

AARP's Life Reimagined initiative is all about helping people to realize that we can choose our path forward at any step in our life's journey. And as a means to that, it enables each of us to connect to a powerful social movement that cuts across traditional distinctions, including age, as we explore together how the future will look for us all.

As someone who has been involved for over a quarter century in the leadership of organizations deeply committed to work that improves the quality of people's lives, I realize how closely people's sense of meaning and fulfillment is tied to their work. I have had the great good fortune of consistently doing work that is closely aligned with my own internal sense of calling. I know how vital it is to be engaged in projects that allow us to express our gifts, in support of causes we are passionate about, with people who share our values and aspirations. That is why I am so excited about this book and so pleased to welcome it as a connected piece in our overall Life Reimagined efforts.

In seeking to discover new life possibilities, it is critical that we develop a clearer sense of the kind of work that gives meaning and purpose to our lives. It does not matter whether we are just graduating college or coming to the end of a lifetime of service to an organization or cause; the same powerful impulse to express who we are through what we do remains alive at every point in our lives.

In this book, you will be led through a journey of self-discovery to help you clarify your own gifts, passions, and values in order to reimagine your work and find meaning and fulfillment. Ultimately, you will uncover that powerful sense of calling that gives our lives meaning no matter where we are on life's journey.

I invite you to experience *Work Reimagined: Uncover Your Calling* as a means to live with a greater sense of purpose, meaning, and joy at every age.

Jo Ann Jenkins
CEO, AARP

Reimagined Lives

Time flies. You get up in the morning, do your thing all day long, and go to bed at night.

Then you wake one day to find that more than two decades have passed—in barely a blink of an eye. Rip Van Winkle himself would be mightily impressed.

The changes that have taken place over the last twenty years or so are staggering: technology that did not even exist in the final part of the twentieth century has come and gone; grey hairs that were only emerging then have achieved dominance and turned white. The external world and its internal counterpart are radically different from then to now as the river of time flows on incessantly.

It is the end of work as we know it. Age-old models of working have broken down in the space of two decades; career paths look nothing like they did in the days before phones got smart.

And yet, there are perennial concerns that have remained steadfast. Questions like "What was I born to do?" and "What is my calling?" continue to intrigue us. The ongoing search for answers and the processes by which we explore are as vital and consuming as ever.

As coauthors and friends, we embarked on a journey together more than twenty years ago. Our first book, *Repacking Your Bags: Lighten Your Load for the Good Life,* represented the initial step in that journey. The central message of *Repacking* was that each of us needs to develop his or her own vision of the "good life"—which we defined as "living in the place you belong, with people you love, doing the right work, on purpose"—and having done so, must then "repack our bags" so that the only burdens we carry are those that really assist us in getting where we want to be.

What we did not fully realize at the time was how much "repacking" would become a vital life skill—not only for us individually, but for us in the broader world of work and relationships as well.

By examining our own lives and asking ourselves the question that started it all in *Repacking:* "Does all this make me happy?" we discovered, individually and together, that many of the choices we had made around place, work, relationships, and purpose were indeed contributing to our overall sense of well-being. But some of them needed to be reimagined and repacked. As a result, we have both made a number of significant changes in our lives—some external and others of a more introspective kind.

Richard reconceptualized his vision of both his executive coaching practice and his work as a partner in *Inventure—The Purpose Company* so that he could focus more on writing and speaking. His deepening understanding of his own sense of purpose and direction has led him to write and collaborate on numerous books and articles, most recently, his coauthorship with Alan Webber of the AARP-supported book *Life Reimagined.*

Dave gave up his career as a corporate consultant to earn a graduate degree in philosophy. For more than a decade now he has been a full-time college teacher, while continuing to pursue his passion for doing philosophy with elementary and middle school students, work that resulted in the publication of his most recent book, *Plato Was Wrong! Footnotes on Doing Philosophy with Young People.*

In the more than twenty years since *Repacking* came out, we have each done a good deal of repacking ourselves. We have both moved several times; Richard remarried and has become fully initiated into the rites of grandparenthood; Dave became a father and has managed to pay off his student loans just in time for his daughter to start accruing hers. Our lives have continued to unfold and to present us with new opportunities for shaping our own visions of the good life.

Through it all, we have carried on the discussion that led to *Repacking.* We have remained deeply intrigued by what it means to live a good life and what people really need to be happy. Our conversations on these issues have ranged far and wide; we have talked with each other, with colleagues and clients, with young children and older adults. To our initial surprise, the one component of the good life that has consistently come to the fore has been work. While we have seen that relationships, place, and purpose are essential to people's overall sense of satisfaction, we have rediscovered the degree to which people's feelings that they are—or are not—doing what they were "meant to do" impacts their overall life fulfillment.

This reality, coupled with what we have learned by interviewing many people who *are* doing what they were meant to, led us in 2001, to write our second book together, *Whistle*

While You Work: Heeding Your Life's Calling. Whereas *Repacking* was centered on an examination of all four components we considered necessary to the good life, *Whistle* focused on the *challenge of discovering meaningful work.*

And now, drawing upon that work and informed by another decade and a half of questioning and reflection, we have come to this book, *Work Reimagined: Uncover Your Calling.* The central notion we explore here is the deep hunger people feel to find meaningful work, work that allows us to express our gifts, and connects us to something larger than ourselves in purposeful ways—in short, the phenomenon of "calling."

Uncovering our calling is what we have found best enables people to experience fulfillment in all phases of their lives. What may be most surprising is that if we can fully embrace our calling and consistently bring it to all that we do, then really for all intents and purposes, we never have to work again—at least insofar as we commonly identify work as something that is a chore, or which we only do to get paid. When we operate from a powerful sense of what we are called to do, then we are not, as the saying goes, simply making a living, we are making a life.

Writing this book together has been another incredible opportunity to express our callings. Each of us, in conducting interviews, facilitating seminars, teaching classes, having discussions, and putting our thoughts on paper has had the great good fortune of using our gifts and expressing our passions in service to something we value deeply. It has been a joyous experience even when—perhaps *especially when*—we were working the hardest. We offer this book as a token of our gratitude for being able to experience the power of calling in our own lives.

In order to live the life we imagine, we must continually re-imagine it. In order to do work that makes such a life possible, we must regularly rediscover and reimagine our calling. Our ongoing conversations about calling have enriched our lives immeasurably and offer every promise of continuing to do so. We welcome you to participate in these conversations yourself and to experience the joy and fulfillment that follows from doing what you are called to do.

Richard J. Leider
Minneapolis, Minnesota

David A. Shapiro
Seattle, Washington

The End of Work As We Know It

Never Work Again

Uncover your calling and you will never have to work again.

By way of illustration, Richard tells the following story:

I settle in to the taxi, hoping to get a bit of work done before my upcoming meeting. As the driver begins pulling away from the curb, I open my briefcase and take out a folder. Even as I try to settle in to my papers, I can see from the cabbie's face in the rearview mirror that he wants to talk.

"So, whattayou in town for?" he asks.

"I'm giving a speech. A presentation to some businesspeople," I say, hoping to make it sound uninteresting so the driver will leave me alone.

He doesn't take the hint. "Oh yeah? What's it about?"

I'm not interested in giving the speech twice, so I offer the Reader's Digest *abridged version. "Hearing and heeding your life's calling—doing the work you were born to do."*

My cabbie scoffs. "That's a good one. You gotta section on how to make a million bucks while you sleep, too?"

Now he's *hooked* me. *"You sound skeptical."*

*"Hey look, what am I supposed to say? Your life's 'calling?'
C'mon, I drive a cab here. What's that got to do with a calling?"*

*I close my folder and catch the driver's eyes in the rearview.
"You weren't born to drive a taxi?"*

He just laughs.

"But you like your work well enough?"

He shrugs. "I guess it has its moments."

"I'm interested. What are those moments?"

"You mean besides quittin' time?"

*I lean forward and put my hand on the back of the seat. "I'm
serious. What is it about this job—besides the money—that you
find satisfying? What is it that gets you out of bed in the morning?"*

*He smirks like he's going to say something sarcastic but then
stops. Gradually, his face softens. He laughs a little and says,
"Well, there's this old lady."*

*I stay silent and he continues. "A couple times a week, I get
a call to pick her up and take her to the grocery store. She just
buys a few items. I help her carry them into her apartment,
maybe unload them for her in her kitchen, sometimes she asks
me to stay for a cup of coffee. It's no big deal, really; I'm not even
sure she knows my name. But I'm her guy. Whenever she calls
for a taxi, I'm the guy that goes."*

I wonder why. "Does she tip well?" I ask.

*"Not really. Nothing special, anyway. But there's something
about helping her that, I dunno, just makes me feel good. I guess
I feel like I'm making a difference in somebody's life, like somebody needs me. I like to help out."*

"There's your calling right there," I say.

"What?" The smirk returns. "Unloading groceries?"

"You said you like to help out. That is a pretty clear expression of calling. 'Giving care to people in need' is how I would probably put it."

A smile spreads across his face. "Well, I'll be damned. I guess that's right. Most of the time, I'm just a driver, but when I get that chance to help somebody—as long as they're not some kinda jerk or something—that's when I feel good about this job. So, whattayou know? I got a calling."

He falls silent for the rest of the short trip. But I can see his face in the rearview mirror and even when we hit the midtown traffic, he's still smiling.

Each of us, no matter what we do, has a calling. Of course, some jobs fit more naturally with our calling, but every working situation provides us with some opportunities for fulfilling the urge to give our gifts away. Satisfaction on the job—and ultimately, in life—will, in part, depend on how well we take advantage of those meaningful moments. What this requires, though, is that we learn to uncover our calling. And in the contemporary world of work, this is no luxury; uncovering our calling is now, more than ever before, an essential life skill.

Do You Have a Job, a Career, or a Calling?

Did Richard's taxi driver see his work as a job? A career? Or a calling? It makes all the difference—especially these days, given new and emerging realities affecting us all.

Once upon a time—let us say the first three-quarters of the previous century—it was not uncommon for people, like the taxi driver, to have the same job their entire lives. A person could expect to work for the same company, in more or less the same capacity, throughout their entire working life.

Later, but still back in the day—let us say the last couple decades of that same end-of-the-millennium century—many, if not most, people had just one career. While particular working situations and companies might come and go, it was typical for someone to be employed in the same capacity in all of them.

Nowadays, though, neither of these is the norm. Hardly anyone works at the same job their entire life—and pretty much no one really expects to. Likewise, even careers are no longer stable. More and more people radically change the direction their working lives take over time. You hear stories every day of doctors giving up their practices to become restaurateurs, computer scientists reinventing themselves as organic farmers, teachers leaving the profession to become tour guides; visit any community college or evening degree program and you will see countless examples of people pursuing very different career dreams than those they started out with.

Moreover, an increasing number of people are doing this simultaneously. The phenomenon of the "slash career," where individuals combine two very different fields of work as part of their identity, continues to rise. No longer is someone merely a lawyer, for example; they are a "lawyer/actress," or an "advertising executive/gluten-free baker," or, as profiled in a featured *New York Times* article, "forensic psychologist/DJ."

The question arises then, as to what can be the consistent thread among these various careers. What draws a person from one field of endeavor to something entirely different? How do we find ourselves? How do we bring the same level of passion and commitment to and derive the same level of satisfaction and meaning from what inevitably seem like unconnected ways of moving through the world?

The answer can be found through an important distinction in how people view their relation to their work as a job, a career, or a calling. People tend to see their work in one of these three ways, and the satisfaction they derive from that work correlates closely.

The Job-Career-Calling Distinction

The distinctions are these: People who have jobs are mainly focused on gaining the material benefits from work. They do not expect to receive any other type of reward from it. The work is not an end in itself, but instead is a means that allows individuals to acquire the resources needed to enjoy their time away from the job. The major life commitments of jobholders are not expressed through their work.

In contrast, people who see what they do as a career have a deeper personal investment in their work and mark their achievements not only through monetary gain, but through advancement within their field. This advancement often brings higher status, increased power, and higher self-esteem.

Finally, people with callings find that their work is inseparable from their lives. A person with a calling works not only for financial gain or career advancement, but also for the fulfillment that doing the work brings to them. The word "calling" was originally used in a religious context where people were understood to be "called" by God to do morally and socially significant work. While the modern sense of "calling" may have lost its religious connection, work that people feel called to do is usually seen as intrinsically valuable—an end in itself.

The Job–Career–Calling distinction is not necessarily dependent upon the kind of work a person does. Within any occupation, one could conceivably find individuals with all three kinds of relations to their work. Although one might expect to find a higher number of callings among those in certain types of work, for example, doctors, teachers, or social service professionals, it is an essential truth that anyone can view their work as a calling. All it takes is that they use their gifts doing something they are passionate about in an environment consistent with their values.

Uncovering our calling, therefore, is key to navigating the changes we will inevitably experience in work. To figure out what we are really called to do in the world is the best means we have of connecting the various aspects of our work lives over time, no matter what our job or career happens to be at the moment.

Taking the Work out of Work

And here is the really good news: when we uncover our calling, we *never have to work again.* That is right. When we choose to do what we are called to do—and we can—then we are always doing what we want to.

And this is not just for people who have "glamorous" jobs with fancy titles and big salaries. A sense of calling enables us to successfully reimagine our work, no matter what we do, as the following story illustrates.

John Novachis never worked a day in his life.

A men's retailer, John was the force behind his small gem of a men's shop in Edina, Minnesota. He hand-selected every piece in his store, every one of which embodied his eccentric and colorful sense of style.

Although he was an icon in the world of men's clothing, his real work was with people; he did what he did for his customers. While handling the fabric of garments, he simultaneously wove himself into the fabric of people's lives. Whether or not you bought anything, John always made you feel like the most important person in the world, regardless of what you did or how much you had to spend.

John was no saint to be sure. He was a profane, outspoken, stereotypically Dionysian Greek, a true Zorba, with a sense of style rivaled only by his sense of humor. He frequently greeted customers entering his store with a robust, "Good f#@&ing afternoon!"

Anyone who knew John would tell you he was one of the happiest and most positive people they had ever met. His philosophy of life was his own version of the "80/20 Rule." He often told Richard, "If you can be happy 80 percent of the time and deal with the crap the other 20 percent, you've got happiness mastered." John himself was at something like 95/5 most days.

John dressed celebrities, athletes, executives, doctors, and men from all walks of life, although you never heard him drop a name. Typically, when referring to someone, well-known or not, he'd proclaim, "I hate that guy!" meaning, of course, "that guy" was someone he was particularly fond of. Everyone was "babe" to John and you could not help but feel honored by and smile at the moniker.

John's calling was "bringing joy" to people's lives, which he also did to the community in which his shop was located. He was named "Merchant of Distinction" by the local business association and there is now a bronze plaque on the building that houses his store, honoring his many contributions.

John was a person who brought all that he was to all that he did—and in doing so, he never had to work a single day in his life.

It is all about uncovering our calling. John designed the life he lived by organizing it around the work he loved to do. This enabled him—as it can for each of us—to commit energetically to activities that lead to fulfillment, and which, from the inside, do not feel like work at all. This is work reimagined at its essence: a reimagining that takes the work out of work!

The Economy of You!

It is the end of work as we know it.

Gone are the days when having a job simply meant "doing your job." No longer can anyone anywhere expect the future of work to be the same as it was in the past. Innovation, which used to be innovative, is now the norm. Staying ahead of the game is what it takes simply to be part of the game.

The last twenty years or so have brought radical revolutions in the way people work. Whereas, for example, two decades ago, telecommuting was relatively novel, today whole industries have sprung up in which customers, suppliers, and producers, are distributed all over the world, connected only by the internet and satellites.

A recent study reveals that one in three members of the American workforce—and a higher percentage of younger workers—are so-called contingent workers, freelancers, temps, seasonal, and part-time employees. That is more than sixty million people, and the numbers are only expected to rise.

This boom marks a striking new stage in a deeper transformation, not just in America, but also around the world. In the twenty-first-century economy, people consistently move among many jobs, organizations, and even careers. Staying put is the anomaly; change is what people call the "new normal," but given how weird things are getting, might better be characterized as the "new abnormal." And that makes reimagining a critical life skill for us all.

More than ever before, people will have to master reimagining to survive in the working world and will have to continue learning to stay up-to-date. They will have to take increased responsibility for educating and re-educating themselves. Individuals will have to learn to "sell" themselves through social networking, and if they are really savvy, turn themselves into "brands." Everyone will feel the pressure to market their most important asset—themselves—and to create and manage what is often referred to as "the economy of you."

Work 1.0: Having a Good Job

The idea that "having a good job" means being an employee of a particular company is a legacy of an era that is ending. The huge companies created by the Industrial Revolution brought armies of workers together, often under a single roof. In its early days, that was a step down for many independent artisans, but a step up for most common day laborers.

These companies, typically combined with the efforts of labor unions, introduced a new stability and security into work. A huge class of white-collar workers found secure positions managing these growing organizations. For much of the twentieth century, working meant a full-time job, which included fringe benefits and a retirement plan. It also meant having a clearly defined job description. Lifelong employment was the expectation, even the "right" of many workers.

But all that has changed. Downsizing, restructuring, new technologies, globalization, automation, robotics, and so on and so on have radically altered the workplace. Nothing looks like it did in the textbooks we studied from. At no other time in human history have so many people had to flip their fundamental assumptions about making a living—to, in essence, reimagine their work lives.

Work 2.0: Having a Calling

How does having a clear sense of calling support working in today's disruptive work world? We answer this question by pointing to a couple of life skills that are essential today: self-awareness and adaptability.

People with a high degree of self-awareness are good at identifying their gifts, passions, and values. They have an accurate sense of their strengths and weaknesses. They can change their self-perception by examining their experiences and getting feedback from others.

Adaptability refers to peoples' capacity to self-regulate—to adjust to the needs of whatever situation they find themselves facing. People with a high degree of adaptability not only have the ability to change, they are motivated to do so. They can sense when they need to update their skills and knowledge and are generally eager to do so.

A clear sense of calling brings with it a heightened sense self-awareness and greater adaptability—along with a continual seeking of ways to better align one's gifts with needs in the world. By cultivating a calling, we are automatically developing a reimagining approach to work that will prove critical to surviving and thriving in the increasingly contingent work world. Those who have identified their calling and who approach their work through that lens will be those with the self-awareness and adaptability to embrace the future of work however it happens to unfold.

The Call for Imagination

The truth is that in today's economy, it is far riskier to abandon your calling than to uncover it.

With the secure job a thing of the past, the only lasting security for any of us lies in our ability to find or create work. We need to continuously reimagine what we do for a living or we risk having life simply pass us by.

The constantly evolving economy rewards people who exhibit qualities like initiative, adaptability, and innovativeness. And who is more likely to embody these qualities than people who believe in and love what they do? Reimagining one's work lies at the root of this.

In today's world of work, those who pursue their calling have a positive edge. They have a powerful source of self-motivation to grow and to take the risks necessary to succeed. On the other hand, those who rely on existing structures to look out for them will soon be left behind.

The riskiest course of action is to wait until a crisis forces us to change. Intentionally reimagining our work, by contrast, enables us to adapt on our own terms. Instead of being limited by circumstances, we are constrained only by what we believe is possible. And the broader the scope of our dreams, the broader will be the range of possibilities before us.

It takes a great deal of imagination and resourcefulness to uncover and heed our calling. But it is imagination that turns color into art, words into poetry, and notes into music. Similarly, it is imagination that turns jobs and careers into callings. As we gather information, open new doors, and explore emerging fields of interest, we feed our imaginations with the essentials we need to uncover our life's work. And as we act, we gain confidence in the work we do, and just as importantly, clarity about why we do it.

One prediction we can be quite sure of: the future of work will be even more different from today than today is from yesterday. Those who are able to continually reimagine themselves for the new realities, while being true to their deepest sense of calling, will be the ones most likely to succeed on their own terms. Historically, fortune has favored the bold; now, more than ever, it will favor the bold reimaginers.

Why Is Reimagining So Vital Today?

Admittedly, some people, especially self-employed people like John Novachis, may have better odds than others of engaging with work through the principle of calling. We are all constrained, in one way or another, by factors such as gender, ethnicity, socioeconomic status, and geography. Economic hardship, in particular, can lead to decreased opportunities for reimagining work.

To be clear, though, all legitimate areas of work provide the possibility of dignity and meaning. There is no type of job that is inherently "better" than some other type. That said, it is an unavoidable reality that people start at different points and the likelihood of reimagining one's work is greater in some situations than others.

But that is only part of the story. The flip side is that for people whose situations are more constrained, calling is even more vital. Paradoxically, having a calling may be most vital for those faced with unemployment or underemployment.

The transition from secure jobs to a more contingent-oriented work world has been evolving steadily over the past half-century, and an adaptive approach to this new reality is now an essential life skill for all of us.

We call this adaptive mindset "work reimagined." When people reimagine, they gain a sense of clarity and confidence by uncovering their calling.

What Is Calling?

We define "calling" as the inner urge to give our gifts away.

We heed our calling when we offer our gifts in service to something we are passionate about in an environment that is consistent with our core values.

Richard has been researching, writing, and speaking about calling for decades—so long, in fact, that when he first began communicating about the concept, he often employed the metaphor of the telephone! The telephone? How archaic is that?

Surprisingly, however, even in this day when the word "telephone" evokes a time of people smoking cigarettes in their offices and taking three martini lunches, the metaphor still has legs. This is primarily because the evolution of the "telephone" over the last few decades illustrates, in no small way, the manner in which our shared understanding of calling has morphed, as well.

It used to be that the place one would receive calls—telephone calls—was fixed. You had to be there when it rang, and if you were not, you missed it. Those of us of a "certain age" probably remember waiting around impatiently for the phone to ring with news about a job or a word from that special someone.

This is akin to how we used to understand calling as well. It seemed to us that the time and place for hearing one's calling was very specific and the call was something we received or did not receive, depending on circumstances. The possibility of missing out on our calling was very real; if we were not fortunate enough to be open to it at the right time, we might be out of luck.

But think of how "telephone" calls have changed over time. These days, with mobile access, satellite connections, texting, tweeting, and so on, we are always in touch. The potential for connection is always there. No one ever has to wait around to be contacted; we can receive the literal call any time, any place.

The same goes for calling in the metaphorical sense. As we now understand calling, we recognize an ongoing, omnipresent, and ubiquitous potential to receive it. At any age or stage in our lives we have the ability to uncover our calling. Our calling is available to us in myriad forms, and our ability to access those forms is virtually limitless. Moreover, the ease of connection provides much more flexibility when it comes to access. We can reimagine our calling and explore it much more freely, in real time, rather than having to dedicate a specific time and place to do so.

That said, there are still a number of principles associated with calling that are as relevant now as they were when phones had rotary dials. These four guiding principles have stood the test of time and help illuminate the timeless nature of the basics of calling:

1) Calling Comes from a Caller

Each and every one of us is called. Where does the call come from? There is no calling without a Caller. Calling is an inherently spiritual concept that challenges us to see our work in relation to our deepest beliefs. The concept of calling is founded on the recognition that we are all born with gifts that enable us to fulfill specific purposes on earth. No one fully understands all that is "hardwired" into newborns, but it is clear that we come into the world already endowed with unique gifts. These gifts have the potential to enrich our lives immeasurably if they are unwrapped and given away. And yet, calling is not revealed to us automatically at birth. Answering our calling requires an effort on our part. Yet, it can be performed almost effortlessly. Quite simply, we must *listen*. We must choose to hear what summons us. We must open ourselves to that inner urge to share our gifts with the world in a meaningful way. When we believe we have a calling—when we have heard the call and can answer it—our full potential for meaningful work can be realized.

2)   Calling Keeps Calling

Calling is revealed to different people at different times in different ways; it may not come to us in a time or a form we expect. Yet we become aware of it by consistent threads that run through our lives: those things we remain passionate about, the work that we continue to believe needs doing in the world. Uncovering our calling is a process that has stages to it, much like the process by which we learned to walk. Each stage—rolling over, crawling, walking, running—had to be experienced in turn. Likewise, we move from *jobs* that pay the bills, to *careers* that help us grow, to *callings* that give us meaning. All three—job, career, and calling—are related, but at different levels and stages, and the common thread that ties them together is the revelation of our calling, if we listen for it.

3)   Calling Is Personal

There are as many callings in the world as there are people on the planet. This is not to say that other people might do the same things that we do or that they cannot be passionate about the identical issues that compel us. It does, however, mean that each of us is called directly; no one else is called to do the same things we are *in the same manner we are.* Our calling is our embedded destiny; it is the seed of our identity. The emphasis here is on *being.* We express calling not only through the work we do, but more importantly, through *whom we are willing to be* in our work. Uncovering our calling involves an intentional choice to be authentic—to uncover in the here and now our true nature. Our calling is like our signature or thumbprint, uniquely ours. Uncovering our calling means we realize that we are here to contribute to life on earth something that no one else can contribute in quite the same way.

4) Calling Is Connection

Uncovering our calling is a deliberate choice to use our gifts to serve others and make a difference in the world. Our calling is made manifest through service to others. We come alive when our efforts make a difference in other people's lives. It is paradoxical but true: we are more likely to receive the meaning and fulfillment we seek when we enable others to achieve the meaning and fulfillment they seek, as well. When what we do is grounded in a sense of calling, we experience a meaning in our work. As a result, we are even more willing and able to connect with others. Calling is thus the connection to our legacy.

These four guiding principles represent the essence of our message about calling. Of course, there's much more to be said about how calling is uncovered and the ways in which we can bring a heightened sense of purpose into our daily lives and work, but the basic idea is quite basic—as we hope to show in the following chapters.

◆ Chapter 1: Reimagining Work—What Do You Do?

In Chapter 1, we explore the question that lies at the root of calling: "What Do You Do?" Here is an opportunity to begin reimagining work in light of it as an expression of who you really are, as opposed to who you think you ought to be. The roots of calling reveal themselves to us at a very young age, In this chapter, you will have the opportunity to reflect upon choices that you have made—and perhaps have not made—to develop a deeper understanding of what you are drawn to, good at, and inspired by.

- **Chapter 2: Reimagining Calling—Should You Quit Your Day Job?**

  Here is where we set a context for reimagining, framed by the *Reimagining Checkup*, a reflective practice to help you consider how to really reimagine your work in terms of calling. You may discover that fulfillment is not always about doing something different, but rather, doing what you do differently.

- **Chapter 3: Reimagining Gifts
  —How Do You Do It?**

  Chapter 3 introduces the Calling Card concept and re-volves around an exploration of your gifts: what am I naturally good at, to what does my hand naturally turn? Each of us has talents and abilities we feel in our bones that we need to use to feel whole. This chapter helps you discover the *how* of work, by helping you identify your gifts in order to be able to apply them fully to work that really matters.

- **Chapter 4: Reimagining Passions
  —Why Do You Do It?**

  Chapter 4 explores the element of inspiration and pur-pose. We are motivated in our work by what we care most deeply about, by those causes that move us, by the people whose needs we are drawn most strongly to serve. In this chapter, you will continue the journey to reimagine work by developing a clearer vision of *why* you work, understood in terms of who the recipients of your efforts really are and are meant to be.

♦ **Chapter 5: Reimagining Values**
—Where Do You Do It?

Chapter 5 investigates the *where* of work by providing ways for you to gain insight into your deepest values and how such commitments foster connections to a working environment that fits. Here will be the opportunity to explore new models of work that provide freedom and autonomy at different phases in your life and career. This will also be a place to investigate and expand upon the importance of what one might call "tribe" in one's work—the vital need to feel a part of a group of people that is moving through the world in ways that are consistent with what we care most about as a group.

♦ **Chapter 6: Reimagining Legacy**
—Have You Played Your Music?

This final chapter explores, in depth, the meaning of success and what a good life really entails. It is really about taking control of our work lives so as to provide ourselves with more autonomy and freedom, even within the context of having too much to do and too little time to do it. The hope is that you come out of this chapter feeling a sense of energy and uplift about your current work and real hope about their relationship to it in the future.

Through these chapters, we intend to provide a process for you to uncover your unique calling. Ultimately, calling is about connecting who we are with what we do.

With this in mind, we welcome you to embark on a journey to reimagine your work as we wonder together about a question that we have heard and wondered about throughout our lives: *What Do You Do?*

CHAPTER 1

....

Reimagining Work— What Do You Do?

The First Question

How soon after you first meet someone do you ask the question? How quickly do others ask you when you first meet: *What do you do?*

It may be the most common question we ask of others and which others ask of us.

It is certainly one of the most important questions we can ask of ourselves: *What do I do? What do I really do? What is my real work?*

Recently, Richard was on a plane trip where he sat next to a businessperson who annoyed passengers as they settled in by talking loudly enough on his mobile phone for everyone to hear. As soon as the plane hit cruising altitude, he asked Richard the standard question: "What do you do?"

Hoping to keep the conversation relatively short, Richard answered quickly, "I'm an author," and turned his attention to his laptop by way of illustration.

"I knew it!" exclaimed the man, "I knew you were somebody! Someday I'd like to write a book myself! That is what I'd like to do!"

At a fundamental level, we all need to feel like "somebody," to do something that gives our life meaning and purpose, some reason to get up in the morning. Work is central to our well-being; what we spend our time doing each day ultimately determines how fulfilled we are. It is not surprising, therefore, that the quest to find fulfilling work is one of the dominant aspirations of people everywhere, at all ages and phases of life.

Nearly all of us spend the majority of our waking lives doing something that we consider "work." Even those who are unemployed, retired, or between jobs have some form of occupation that engages them, be it looking for a job, doing volunteer service, or simply taking care of things around the house.

When people first meet, they almost inevitably ask each other, "What do you do?" If we can answer that question with something we find fulfilling, we are likely to be fulfilled in other areas of our lives, as well. The inevitable question that then arises is, How can we find work that we find fulfilling? The answer to that lies in uncovering our calling. And when we are able to do that, we come to better understand not only what we are meant to do, but even more fundamentally, we develop a better sense of who we really are.

What Do You Want To Be When You Grow Up?

When we were kids, we imagined what work would be like when we grew up. When parents and teachers asked us what we wanted to be, we usually had a ready answer. "A doctor. A firefighter. An explorer." We envisioned a life of excitement and challenge on the job—a life in which we would employ our best-loved talents on projects we were passionate about.

For many of us, though, it has not exactly worked out that way. We find ourselves in working situations that are far from what we envisioned as children. Our jobs are *just jobs*. They pay the bills, but they do not provide us with the whistle in our work. Even worse, we have forgotten what we wanted to be when we grew up.

So maybe it is time to ask ourselves again:

What do I want to be when I grow up?

With that in mind, perhaps it is time to take a lesson from a group of sixth-graders Dave worked with in a Seattle middle school. To a student, they all had very strong feelings about what the future ought to hold for them—and even stronger feelings about what it ought not. Each of them had already answered the question we are still asking:

What do I want to be when I grow up?

Dave tells about an incident that made this abundantly clear to him, in a way that helped him realize what his own answer finally was.

We are playing a game called "Hand Dealt," which explores the question, "Is life fair?" by providing each player with a predetermined "life." Students are each dealt three cards: one determines a fictional relationship they are in, one establishes a fictional job or jobs, and the third tells them where they live. There is a wide range of relationships, occupations, and accommodations, from the quite affluent to the extremely poor. Thus, one player may end up having been dealt a "life" made up of two parents, one of whom is a chemical engineer making $80,000 a year, the other of whom is a banker earning $125,000 annually, two kids, living in a four-bedroom house, while another player is dealt a "life" as an unemployed single parent of four children living in a one-bedroom apartment. Not surprisingly, the kids who get the "good" lives tend to respond to the question of life's fairness in the affirmative, while those who are dealt less desirable lives usually respond that life is horribly unjust. This gives us the opportunity to wonder aloud about the relationship between monetary success and happiness, and ultimately, about just what it means for life to be fair or unfair.

But that is not all. It also gives us a chance to explore what it feels like to be dealt a life we did not choose. This, more than anything else, is what energizes our discussion. The kids are adamant about the injustice of having to live with choices they did not make.

"I wouldn't mind being a janitor," says a boy I'll call Carlos, whose bleached-blond surfer look belies an unusual level of thoughtfulness for an eleven-year-old, "if being a janitor is what I wanted to be. But since it isn't my choice, I don't think it's fair."

But the cards were passed out fairly, weren't they? Didn't everyone have an equal opportunity to be whatever they ended up being?

"That is not the point," says Miranda, a rather small girl with a rather large personality. "What makes it fair or not is that it's your own life and that nobody's forced you into it."

"Yeah. Some people are actually happy being, I dunno, schoolteachers. But that for me would be like worse than prison." This comment from Will, one of the class's several class clowns elicits a humorous grimace from his teacher and chuckles from his classmates.

"Could you imagine coming to school for the rest of your life?" shouts curly-haired Maya with a theatrical shiver. "What a disaster!"

Amidst the general assent of her fellow students, I wonder out loud what kinds of things these eleven- and twelve-year-olds could imagine doing for the rest of their lives. I am taken aback at the assurance with which they respond.

"When I grow up, I'm going to be a movie director," says Erin, a seemingly shy girl who spends much of her time drawing. "I'm going to start by doing commercials and then videos and then feature films."

Ryan, who collared me the moment I entered the classroom to show me his daily journal, in which he is recording tidbits for the autobiography he is working on, pipes up that he's going to be a writer. "Maybe I can write your movie scripts," he says to Erin.

Other students have similarly well-formed notions of what they love doing. I am enjoying immensely talking to them about what they plan to do, how they plan to do it, and what are the philosophical implications of their choices—and their freedom to make those choices. I wonder how they manage to have such optimism and clarity about their lives at this point. I also wonder how—at this age—they seem to know themselves so well. When did they have the discovery that so often eludes adults: the discovery of what they want to be when they grow up?

Suddenly, I come to understand that I am having that same discovery myself. As I stand in a classroom, doing philosophy with children, I realize that finally, after years of searching, I am at last doing what I most love to be doing. All the other jobs I have ever had—from busboy to videodisc designer to corporate training consultant—have been merely steps upon the way to where I am now. I feel completely connected to the process of inquiry we are conducting; I am immersed in the subject matter and delighted by my young colleagues and their inquiring minds. Time flies by. What I notice is how authentic it feels for me to be helping these students to better understand the questions and answers we are exploring, and in the process, to better understand themselves. It occurs to me that in all the other jobs I have ever had, this is the common theme that has given me satisfaction. At some level, "creating dialogue" is what has consistently been key.

And I realize that after many years, I've finally become what I always wanted to be when I grew up. It has taken me half a century to find the answer to the question that my young friends in this classroom have found for themselves in just over a decade: What do you want to be when you grow up?

The Roots of Calling

At a fairly young age—by fifth or sixth grade, certainly—many of us have some sense of what we love to do—and what we do not. Of course, we cannot put a job title on it at that point; loving to draw does not translate into being an art director for an eleven-year-old. Nor is finding math class fun a sign that a youngster should think about becoming an accountant. Moreover, given that well over half of the jobs kids will grow up and go into have not even been invented yet, it is obvious that we cannot expect too much specificity in career choice at such a young age.

Still, the essential roots are already there. Our gifts, though nascent, have already begun to take shape. Deep within, a part of us knows that we are here on this planet for a reason. A sense of destiny, unformed as it is, lies just beneath the surface of our awareness. And even as children, we naturally incline toward the experiences that allow us to express this.

Somewhere along the line, though, we get sidetracked. We silence that voice within that speaks to us about what really matters. We make choices—or have them made for us—that are driven by practical concerns. We set aside "childish" dreams in the interest of making a living or satisfying someone else's dream. We seem to forget what we knew as boys and girls—what we most love to do.

But that wisdom never really goes away. It can be revived. We can open ourselves to that innate reimagining that guided us when we were young: the inner urge to give our gifts away.

The roots of calling in our lives go back very deeply—perhaps to even before we were born. Calling is an expression of our essence; it is our embedded destiny. The seed of this destiny lies within us, and seeks, one way or another, to fulfill itself in the world. So the question we need to ask ourselves is whether we are doing all we can to bring the fruits of our calling to bear.

Seeds of Destiny

One unmistakable conclusion that Richard has drawn from a lifetime of coaching individuals about life and career design is this: *we all possess seeds of destiny.* Each of us has within us innate natural gifts—unique potential for creative expression. From birth we have what we need to become all we can be. The challenge, of course, is to figure out how to make a living with our uniqueness, how to connect who we are with what we do.

Often, we do not have to look very far to find our life's calling. We can simply start doing whatever we are already doing—driving a taxi, being a lawyer, raising a child, waiting on tables—with greater awareness and expression of our natural gifts.

On a day-to-day basis, we always have the choice to bring more of ourselves—our gifts—to what we do. These choices are meaningful because we do them with a feeling of purpose rather than simply to earn a paycheck. They are naturally rewarding and often occur effortlessly. Such moments put a whistle in our work. They fill purposeful lives—lives that are apt to be happier than lives that lack such moments.

The way we approach our work depends on our "big picture" of life. Unfortunately, many of us lose that perspective; we get so focused on the hand we were dealt that we make decisions impulsively, losing touch with what is really important to us. Ironically, if we can find a moment or means to widen our focus to that longer view, we may discover that what we are looking for is already within sight.

Acorns and Elocution

A sense of calling lies deep within us all. Each of us is, you could say, like an acorn. Somehow, almost magically, the acorn knows how to grow up to be an oak tree. It does not matter where you plant it, whether you put it in an oak forest, an orange grove, or even a junkyard, as long it gets the necessary sunlight and water, the acorn will develop into an oak tree. The acorn's destiny to flourish as an oak is implanted within itself. Attempting to make the acorn grow into a pine tree, for instance, will be—at best—fruitless; more likely, it will destroy the tree altogether.

The same can be said for our own destinies. Like the acorn, each of us contains within us the power to realize the fullest expression of who we are. Naturally, we need a good environment in which to grow and thrive, but assuming we can cultivate that, we can grow our roots down and reach up to become tall and mighty in our own way.

Sadly, many of us spend our lives trying to grow our acorns into pine trees—or palms or sycamores or something even more exotic and unlikely, and this stunts our growth. Yet our destiny continues to seek fulfillment in becoming an oak tree. Small wonder so many of us grow up feeling rather gnarled and twisted. Small wonder so many of us end up making work or lifestyle choices that hinder our natural growth.

One of the most common messages many young people receive is that they should rein in their natural creative capacities. How many of us have heard "You can't sing," You can't draw," or "You're not a writer"? How many of us were told we were not good in one or all of the creative arts? And even those of us lucky enough to have had our creativity supported, were likely to have been told that we could never make a living as a singer or artist or poet. Each time these limitations were imposed upon us, most of us acted as if they were the truth. We accepted the limitations, imposed them upon ourselves, and thus, the limitations became real.

The lesson is that when we are given strong positive messages about our natural abilities, we tend to bring them forth quite successfully. Those of us fortunate enough to have had parents or mentors who encouraged our creative expression often find ourselves using those very abilities in our work lives as adults. Richard, for instance, who now makes a good deal of his living by giving speeches had programmed into him from a very young age the simple message "You can speak." He bought it.

"When I was a preteen," says Richard, "my father strongly encouraged me to get up early every morning and look up a new word in the dictionary. At breakfast, I would share from memory my new word with him. I always picked ones that I thought would impress him—words like 'ameliorate' or 'erudition.' He believed that to be successful in any work or in life you needed to be able to express yourself clearly and articulately. For him, having the vocabulary to say precisely what you meant with a certain poetic flourish was a vital component of success. Encouraging me to learn a 'word a day' was how he impressed upon me the importance of this.

"His next push was for me to take elocution lessons. I dreaded this. My friends would be playing hockey at the corner playground on Saturday mornings while I sat with Miss Loker learning how to speak. Miss Loker was a dowdy, gray-haired woman in her seventies who seemed plucked directly from the musty volumes of English literature that she carried with her for my lessons. Always perfectly put-together and freshly coifed, she showed up on Saturdays with poems to be memorized and lessons on pronunciation and inflection to be learned. I would avoid the work she gave me all week long and try to cram it all in on Friday afternoon. Consequently, I dreaded her visits and the inevitable humiliation of having to stand before her, in my own living room, reciting the week's lesson over and over and over.

"The true terror, though, was the recital, six months out, where she brought all her students together in an auditorium to recite their selected piece. For months, I came up with every conceivable excuse to avoid this event. Unfortunately, there was no way out. I ended up on stage before scores of expectant parents, reciting my piece under the stark glow of the theater lighting. Much to my surprise, I liked it. Hearing my voice reverberate through the hall and seeing the smiles and hearing the applause of the audience gave me a thrill I never forgot.

"As a sensitive and mostly introverted thirteen-year-old, elocution lessons did not help me get picked for hockey games on Saturday afternoons or be able to talk to girls at school. But they did teach me to be comfortable speaking in front of groups. In fact, after two years of lessons, I found within me a natural enjoyment for sharing stories in front of a live audience. I discovered that I had a gift for communicating my thoughts and feelings to groups of people.

"Today I make much of my living sharing stories and lessons learned with audiences of all sizes. Speaking in public is a part of my work that I truly enjoy. It brings forth the whistle in my work.

"I often wonder if my parents saw this natural inclination of mine for public speaking or whether they just felt it would be a good skill for me to acquire. In any case, they nurtured my gift for it, and in doing so, helped make it possible for me to make a living doing what I love to do."

Doing What You Love, Not What You Should

How many of us ended up where we are because someone— probably a parent or a teacher —"should'ed" us? Somewhere along the line, a mentor of some sort told us that we *should* go into some line of work or some course of study "to make a good living" or because some other occupation "isn't practical," or so we can have "something to fall back on," if what we *really* love to do does not work out?

You see it all the time with college students. An eighteen-year-old freshman loads up his schedule with lots of math and science, even though what he really loves is theater. If he is lucky, about the time he is a junior, he realizes he has made a mistake and changes his major. If he is not lucky, he ends up graduating and taking a job that makes him miserable.

Dave remembers a young woman who took an Introduction to Philosophy course from him. "She was quite good at it. She had a natural knack for understanding the often quite difficult arguments of the philosophers we were reading. She seemed to really enjoy the interplay of ideas in the classroom; she wrote great papers, and often came to my office hours to discuss philosophical questions. Given her enthusiasm for the material, I naturally assumed she was majoring in philosophy. But no, she said, she was pre-med. 'Well, then you'd better watch out,' I joked, 'given your talent, if you're not careful, you're going to end up a philosophy major.' She just laughed.

"After the class, I lost track of her and did not see her again until about two years later, when we happened to meet by chance in the library. I asked her how her studies were going, what courses she was taking and so on. She listed the classes she was enrolled in that quarter—they were all upper division philosophy courses!

"'I thought you were pre-med,' I said.

"'I switched to philosophy,' she told me.

"I kidded her about the comparative job prospects of a

philosopher and a physician. 'Well, your parents must have been delighted about that!'

"She laughed, 'Yeah, I thought when they found out I changed, they were going to kill me.' Then she got serious, 'But, I thought that if I didn't change, I might kill myself.'"

The message is this: we limit ourselves by doing what we think we *should do.* But by doing what we *love to,* we expand our potential and increase the likelihood that the work that we do will be consistent with our gifts. We maximize our chances for whistling while we work.

Nobody but you knows what your path should be. Maybe it means taking a job as a taxi driver. Perhaps it is to go to the seminary or teach philosophy to children. Maybe expressing your calling means to form a collectively owned organic farm, or maybe it is to run for mayor of your small town. Or perhaps you will heed your calling to become a chef, a poet, or teacher. There are thousands of callings and limitless ways to express them—and only we can name our calling and act upon it.

People who are fulfilled in their work tend to have exercised choice in getting where they are. They usually have—at some point or another—taken the proverbial "bull by the horns" and set a direction for their lives. They tend to have pursued that direction, using their intuition as a compass to navigate with. This is not to say they necessarily travel in a straight line—they may change course many times along the way—but the mere fact of choosing their life's course enables them to purposefully pursue their dreams. And the sense of power that comes from knowing that their direction is freely chosen provides them with the impetus to continue choosing throughout their lives.

It is a useful exercise, therefore, to look back on our own lives and think about the twists and turns that led us to where we are today. What were the key choices we made—or did not make— that resulted in our becoming the person we are, with the work we have, living in the place we do, with the people we know?

The Role of Role Models

The attitudes toward work of the adults who influenced us as children form the foundation upon which we build our own perspective. The way that our parents and other influential grownups worked—and talked and thought about work—are the first images we had of the working world, and, therefore, have a deep and powerful influence on our own attitudes.

Growing up, we generally formed opinions about work by observing the behavior and listening to the words of our elders. Our parent or parent figures—the most important people in our lives—modeled to us the meaning of work. Our own relationship to work evolved from that starting point.

For some of us, Dad was the parent who most clearly characterized the nature and meaning of work. For others, it was Mom, and for many, it was both—or some other significant person in our lives. If our role model—whoever they were— whistled while they worked, saw work as joy, we are more likely to seek enjoyment in our own work. If they saw their jobs as drudgery, as only a way to pay the bills, we are more likely to want to avoid it.

Of course, our beliefs and attitudes about work are complex and have their origins in many sources, but usually, observing the work lives of our parent figures forms the basic pattern.

Richard, for instance, observed his father and formed the foundation of his perspective on calling. "My father was a banker, an executive who worked for the same organization for thirty-nine years. He worked hard—got up early in the morning six days a week to go to the office. He did so not simply to make a living, but because he believed that his efforts had a positive effect on individuals and the St. Paul, Minnesota, community. This symbolic message, that work is a way to make a difference in people's lives, is deeply programmed into me. The bright side of what my father modeled to me about work was his masterful ministry to people. When I went to his office and saw him relate to people or we walked together down the streets of St. Paul, it was obvious that he was very skillful and enjoyed what he was doing. He whistled while he worked. He created the aura of an artist when he worked, echoing the words of Suzuki, who wrote, "I am an artist at living and my work of art is my life." I learned from my father that through following the inner urge to give your gifts away you find your true self.

For those of us not so lucky to have role models like Richard, however, the good news is that we are not trapped by the past. If we can recognize the source of our attitudes towards work, we are in a position to change them. Just because we grew up in a household, for instance, where the influential adults saw work as a necessary evil, does not mean we are condemned to share that perspective. We can challenge what we were taught as children and form our own more positive relationship with work. It starts with interrogating the messages we received and then revising them to be more consistent with work that is meaningful and fulfilling.

Consider how many of us were brought up to believe that we could not possibly make a living doing what we enjoy. We have a choice: either we can enjoy what we do or we can eat!

But step back for a moment and ask yourself if this makes sense. Is it true? Are all the people you know who enjoy their work starving?

Growing up, lots of us were told by well-meaning adults that work is not something to be enjoyed. "It's not supposed to be fun; that is why they call it work." Messages like that made a powerful impression, which was reinforced by seeing grownups drag themselves off to their jobs, complaining all the way.

Imagine, by contrast, that we all heard a message like this when we were young: *"Welcome, my child! You've been born into an exciting era with unlimited potential. We don't know what your innate gifts are, but we're committed to helping you discover them. We could never see the world thorough your eyes because you were born to be you and to live a life that is yours alone to live. You have gifts that will come to you so naturally that no one can teach you how to use them, not even us! Your gifts will give you untold joy and will be as easy for you as breathing. We will give you plenty of chances to explore what you really enjoy doing in order for your gifts to truly flourish. We'll be proud of and celebrate whatever calling you choose for yourself, whatever it is that makes you happy."*

How much easier it would be for people to uncover their unique, life-inspiring calling!

So why not try it out? Why not imagine that you have been told all along that you are here for a purpose and that a key aspect of this is to discover what your purpose really is? It is not so hard to accept this as a starting point—and ultimately, it is far easier on us than believing the alternative.

Take it as a given, at least experimentally: Our callings exist within us; they are inborn, a natural characteristic, like our hair color or whether we are right- or left-handed. But until we uncover our calling, we are not living authentically; we are adopting someone else's model for who we should be. Perhaps it is who our parents thought we should be; perhaps it is a false image that we ourselves have opted for. In any case, that false image must be examined, reevaluated, and reimagined if we are to live lives of meaning and purpose.

Each of us has a unique and special calling. *What is yours? What is your special role to perform in life's great drama?*

Connecting Who You Are With What You Do

Calling is proactive. It seeks expression in the world.

Historically, calling has been about the spiritual life. Preachers, evangelists, missionaries, and clergypeople speak about being "called" to do God's work. "Calling" in this sense was deeply rooted in a theological tradition and typically excludes the vast majority of people who are not similarly called.

But there is a more inclusive, secular sense of calling, a sense to be found in the word "vocation." Vocation comes from the Latin *vocare,* meaning "to summon." Here we are referring to the inner urge, or summoning, we have to share our uniqueness with others. In this sense, everyone has a calling, not just those involved in the religious world. Each of us has something—or perhaps several things—that we are, it seems, quite literally called upon to give. We feel a strong pull in a certain direction and our lives seem incomplete unless that direction is pursued.

In this way, calling is *active.* It is a summons to play our part. Calling is a present moment notion; it is alive in our lives all the time. The pull of calling tugs on us during our entire lifetime.

Although calling runs through our whole lives, we are not called once for life. It is something we do every day. Calling breaks down into daily choices. Responding to our calling, we ask ourselves again and again: "How can I consistently bring who I am to what I am doing?"

We have the potential to bring our calling to life every single day. And we do so by expressing our gifts, passions, and values in a manner that is consistent with the impact we want to have.

People who have discovered their calling and choose to bring it to their work tend to be phenomenally energized about what they do. They have an almost childlike passion for their projects and a great sense of gratitude for their good fortune. They have answered the eternal question we face everyday: "Why do I get up in the morning?" And they have answered it by aligning who they are with what they do.

"It's for You"

Inside each of us right now is a call waiting to be answered. It has been with us for all of our lives. The call was placed the moment we were born; it has been ringing in the background every day we have lived.

Taking that call—hearing and heeding our calling—is not the easiest path through life, but it is a path of fulfillment. It is a path of satisfaction quite different from the traditional world of jobs and careers most of us grew up with. If we are going to find fulfillment in our work, we will do so by approaching it as a calling. And if we feel unfulfilled, it is clear that we have yet to make that approach.

Some people discover a sense of calling in fairly dramatic ways: through sensing an inner voice, in a vision, from a dream, as a result of a near-death experience, a shamanic journey, or meditative insight. For others, the call comes more subtly: through an inner knowing, a felt sense that "it fits," or an overall perception of "rightness." Sometimes calling is revealed by a process of elimination, through the turns and dead ends of life. In some instances, a teacher's influence is central; sometimes it is a book or a lecture or the example of others. Some people report gaining insight about their calling through religious revelation or while traveling to new places. In many instances, our callings come once we are removed from the setting of our everyday routines—when we have the opportunity to listen inwardly to what authentically moves us.

Unlocking one's calling requires an inward journey. Each one of has unique potential—distinct, innate gifts—with which to serve the world. These gifts provide us with a source of identity in the world, but until we connect who we are with what we do, that source remains untapped.

Some people are lucky enough to easily hear their calling and naturally find work that allows them to express it fully. But what about the rest of us who listen for our calling but do not hear a thing? Or hear conflicting things? What if I'm in a job that pays well, but brings me little joy? Or a job that pays poorly and provides a sense of fulfillment? What good is a calling if I am trapped in a dead-end job?

All of us go through periods when our work feels dead and lifeless. All of us have dreamed of winning the lottery and never having to work again. Similarly, most of us also have had some opportunities to feel the joy that follows from doing work that is an expression of our deepest nature. Yet when it comes to reimagining our work, most of us have the cards stacked against us. Naming our calling—and more importantly, getting *paid* for living it—seems as unlikely as winning the lottery.

Nevertheless, right here, right now, there are ways to reimagine work. The challenge is to find and create those aspects of your work that express your calling—even if the work as a whole leaves something to be desired.

Uncovering our calling does not mean that we should immediately quit our day jobs. It does, however, require us to work the process of connecting who we are with what we do.

Ultimately, the realization of our calling can occur anywhere. No special circumstances are necessary; what matters is a willingness to recognize the call when it occurs, even if our intuition seems to be guiding us in an unexpected direction.

Uncovering our life's calling means thriving, not just surviving. It means that we refuse to accept less than full engagement of our talents. It means not settling for a relationship with our work that lacks passion.

The Story of Your Story

The way we process the events in our lives through language makes a huge difference. The same incident, described in two different ways, becomes two different incidents.

Think about the story you tell yourself about a day at work. To the question, "What do you do?" you may answer in any number of ways: "Making a living," "Contributing to the success of my organization," "Just putting in time," "Supporting my family." All of these may be equally true depending on the story you are telling. But what is critical to notice is that your description of what is happening will contribute to that description's accuracy. The story we tell ourselves makes that story come true.

What this means is that we can effect real change in our personal and professional lives by changing the stories we tell ourselves. We can understand ourselves better by better understanding our personal narratives. By rewriting the stories we tell ourselves about who we are and what we do, we can reimagine our lives in ways that make it possible to write in more happiness, success, and fulfillment.

An effective first step in this rewriting process is to retrace our steps. How did we get where were are? What choices did we make or not make? How did events transpire such that we are doing what we are doing today? Did we choose our work or did it choose us?

Dave's story illustrates what we mean.

"I can't say I ever made a conscious decision to become a writer," he admits. "Writing was just something I'd always done. From the time I was about eleven, I kept a journal; I always liked corresponding by mail with friends; and in school, I was that weird kid who actually enjoyed English composition class. But it never really occurred to me that I could make a living writing, that doing what came so naturally could actually be a career choice. So, for the first part of my life, I considered writing more of an avocation than a vocation; I wrote for fun, without any real prospect of making money off of it.

"In my early twenties, more or less on a lark, I wrote a few pages of jokes for a stand-up comedian who was appearing at a club near my apartment in Los Angeles. Much to my surprise, he liked some of them, and eventually *paid me* for a few. It wasn't much, but it gave me a taste of earning money for doing what I liked best.

"So it was basically an accident that I started writing for a living and even more of a fluke that I ever got a full-time job doing it."

"It was through the writing of *Repacking Your Bags* with Richard that the disconnect around my calling emerged for me. I realized that while I loved writing and that while putting words together represented the primary manner in which I sought to make a difference in the world, a writer wasn't actually what I wanted to be when I grew up. Writing was part of it—a big part—but it was really just a means to an end that, for me, was really about promoting understanding. I came to see that what I was consistently drawn to wasn't actually the words, it was what those words could do. And when I had the experience of helping people to understand things that helped them understand themselves better, this is when I really came alive. Oddly enough, this "a-ha" led me to, among other things, graduate school, a career in academia, and the work I currently do exploring philosophy with college and pre-college students. More importantly, it led me to finally becoming what I wanted to be when I grew up."

"Looking back over my life—retracing my path—enables me to see the steps and missteps that led me to where I am today. It gives me insight into the manner in which I made choices—or let them be made for me—and helps me consider ways I might have chosen differently, or better. Above all, it is clear to me from looking back that I made a lot of mistakes. I often took jobs that didn't suit me. Time and again I found myself involved in projects that were a poor match for my skills and interests. A lot of time and energy was wasted; a lot of sleep was lost.

"I often wonder what would have happened had I been clearer about what I was looking for from the start. It is easy to imagine the struggles I would have avoided had I not spent so much time spinning my wheels. I might have arrived where I am today with many fewer difficulties and far more satisfaction. It has all worked out in a way, but it could have happened with a lot less confusion and effort."

Of course, some measure of confusion and extra effort is inevitable. Life is unpredictable; none of us really knows where we are going to end up until we get there. But having a process helps—and the one that follows in subsequent chapters works, if you work the process.

CHAPTER 2

······························

Reimagining Calling—
Should You Quit Your Day Job?

The Perfect Job

When people are introduced to the idea of reimagining work, it is not uncommon for them to respond in something like the following way: "It sounds great in theory, but I think I should be grateful just to have a job. I'm just trying to get by, doing what it takes to make ends meet. I know there is more to life than this, but I can't see what it is or how to get it. I'm working harder than ever, but somehow, I'm accomplishing less. I'm stressed out and the problem is that all the alternatives—changing my career, starting over, finding something different—seem overwhelming. How can I trade the security of my job for the uncertainty of a fresh start? I feel guilty even thinking about the luxury of meaningful work. My parents would never have complained in this way."

Does this sound familiar at all?

Few of us really have the "luxury" of having the perfect job—the one that really engages our gifts, where we are only focused on projects we are passionate about, and where the culture is consistent with our deepest values. But even if we do not experience that ideal, we do have the "luxury" of choosing how we experience our work. We have some control—not complete freedom perhaps, but some choice over what parts of our job we focus on and thus, some degree of control over what our work is like.

We can, for example, focus on how our work is making a difference, no matter how small, in other people's lives. Or, we can appreciate the opportunity our work gives us to develop or expand our talents. If we have trouble finding intrinsic meaning in our job, we can remind ourselves that it provides for us and those we care about, or that it enables us to do things that feel meaningful when we are not on the job.

It is a well-known phenomenon, and one which research supports, that people who make the choice, consciously our not, to see their work as "just a job" without connecting it to some larger purpose, are less happy and less satisfied with their lives than are those who view their work as a calling. If you identify yourself in that group, there are really only two viable options: *finding work that is meaningful* or *finding meaning in your work.*

Meaningful Work *or* Meaning In Work

If the first option is outside most of your control, then it is really the second that offers the most fruitful opportunity.

But how do you get started?

Consider what we call *The Work Reimagined Checkup.* Just as our physical health benefits from a periodic assessment, so does our mental health. We invite you therefore, to reflect on the following list; if three or more of the statements below are true for you, then a fuller reimagining of your work may be in order.

The Work Reimagined Checkup

- Life seems to be passing me by while I am trying hard to make a living.

- Work is getting my best energy, and my relationships are getting what is left.

- I know there is more to work, but I am not sure what it is or how to get it.

- I am ready to take my career in a new direction, but I do not know what it is or how to figure it out.

- These days, I rarely wake up eager to face the workday with anticipation and energy.

- I rarely enjoy what I do each day on the job.

- I do not feel like my gifts and talents are being used well at work.

- I rarely go to sleep at night with a fulfilling sense that this has been a well-lived day.

How did you do? How many statements were true for you? How many do you feel you can change? Your answers to these questions can help you frame the way you reimagine your work and help provide an impetus for making changes that can lead to greater engagement and fulfillment.

Finding Meaning In Work

After reflecting on *The Work Reimagined Checkup,* it may become apparent that, for the most part, passion and purpose are not to be found by changing jobs; they are to be found within your current job. Meaningful work is not primarily something that lies outside of us; we have to first discover it inside. If we cannot locate it in ourselves, right where we are in the current moment, it is far less likely we will find it elsewhere.

But here is the secret that is not so secret: Once we are able to reveal to ourselves the core of calling, our jobs can begin to transform themselves—and what we are seeking seems to almost miraculously appear. Our calling has little to do, in fact, with a particular job and everything to do with how we approach it. Any honest and legitimate area of work can potentially be a place to express our calling.

In short, there is no such thing as meaningful work; the meaning is what we bring to it.

And that is what reimagining work is all about.

What's the Risk of Not Reimagining?

You do not really have time to think about that, do you? At least not if, like so many of us today, you are suffering from "hurry sickness"—always going somewhere, never being anywhere. High-stress, high-velocity living with constant deadlines, fast food, power naps, and speed dating makes it difficult to pause and savor the passing moments of our lives. The result is "burnout."

Burnout is the cumulative result of stress resulting in a state of physical, emotional, and mental exhaustion.

Stressed people have plenty of pressure and demands but know they can get through it. Stress is often short-term and situational. Once the situation changes, stress often lets up or goes away for a while. Burned out people are under stress with the same pressures and demands, yet they lack the resilience to get through it.

While it is easy to spot in others, seeing the signs of burnout in oneself is more difficult. It creeps up on you unexpectedly. You may be so busy working that you fail to notice (or pretend not to notice) your own symptoms.

Some additional symptoms of burnout include: trouble sleeping, feeling empty, being absent often from events, experiencing minor illness often, being irritated easily, pulling away emotionally from others, and, simply, joylessness.

Also, self-medicating by using alcohol, drugs, food, or shopping in order to feel better (or perhaps to feel numb) is a key sign of burnout.

If these early signs of burnout remind you of depression, you are right. Depression is quite similar. In fact, burnout has the potential to put some people at increased risk for depression, anxiety, and other emotional issues.

Job burnout comes from feeling like we are doing too much that does not employ our gifts. Or, that we are spinning our wheels on work that we are not passionate about. Or, that we are spending all our time in an environment that is a poor fit for our values. In short, burnout is a direct result of feeling too overwhelmed to really uncover our calling.

The Death of Purpose

While job stress can lead to burnout, burnout can lead to "Inner Kill." Inner Kill is the death of purpose.

Inner Kill people have lost hope. Losing hope leads to Inner Kill. Inner Kill is giving up on the situation or yourself. It is losing hope that things will get better. It is resignation. It is the death of self-respect, and, ultimately, of purpose in life.

Some symptoms of Inner Kill include: avoiding decisions; daydreaming about early retirement; talking a lot about what you are going to do, but doing nothing; lying awake at night, sleepwalking by day; two weekly visits to the liquor store, when one used to be enough; finding yourself talking to friends about the same things week after week.

Inner Kill becomes chronic when you find yourself going through "the motions" instead of being engaged. Over time, this leads to hopelessness—giving up control of your life to whatever or whoever is around you. Burnout is over-doing. Inner Kill is under-being.

Inner Kill comes from feeling like we are not using our gifts in support of things we care about, or that we are stuck in an environment that is inconsistent with our values. In short, Inner Kill is a direct result of feeling disconnected from our calling.

Are you experiencing burnout or Inner Kill? Both? Should you consider quitting your day job? Or is there another way to get out of it?

Getting out of It and Getting into It

The ultimate solution to avoiding burnout is to "unlock the power of purpose." Look at the deeper impact of what you do every day. How does your work make life better for other people? How could you "give" to others? What might you achieve if you decided to dedicate years, rather than months, to something? What project can you start that might sustain your passion for a lifetime?

Richard has seen firsthand how people can get stuck in situations they feel are inescapable. He recalls an incident that showed him what we believe is the only way out.

Africa—at last!

I have always dreamed of coming here. And now, I've finally made it, invited by Derek Pritchard, Executive Director of the Voyageur Outward Bound School, and former director of the Kenya Outward Bound School on the slopes of Mount Kilimanjaro. Derek is leading a group of seasoned outdoorspeople— Outward Bound leaders and board members—on this East African adventure. Little do I know that the real excitement and growth on our trip will be the inner journey—the "inventure."

We are taking a route that is particularly challenging, but this group wants to "push the envelope," to have an authentic African safari experience. And so, we find ourselves with full backpacks in a remote area along the eastern edge of the Serengeti Plain, climbing up from the Great Rift Valley—scrambling along the great Rift itself—as we make our way forward under the brutal African sun. Our goal is to hike across the Salei Plain to the Ngorongoro Crater where we will meet the truck that left us several days ago. None of us have taken this route before; it is new even to our Masai guide, so we are unsure of what lies ahead, nervous about our limited water supplies holding out.

Animals are everywhere; hyenas' yelps are a constant counterpoint to our own sounds of labored breathing and heavy footfalls. There are ten people in our group—men and women—and we are mostly silent, conserving our energy for the trek ahead. Our thoughts do not stray far from the experience at hand; ancient fears of the wild continent we are trekking cross abound.

At the moment, we have good reason to be on edge. We are hiking through tall grass that obscures our view beyond just a few paces. It is called, appropriately enough, "lion grass," because it is a favorite habitat of lions on a hunt. They hunker down in the dry stalks to hide from their prey, ready to spring up when an unsuspecting animal comes across their line of sight.

Our group is spread out in a line behind our guide. I am near the rear, taking my time, trying to experience each moment of our trip as fully as I can. The only other member of our brigade that I can see, occasionally through the tall grass, is a man I will call 'Tom,' a fairly experienced hiker, an Outward Bound board member, who in the 'real world' is an extremely successful New York City attorney. Tom is on his first trip to Africa, too, and seems even more blown away by the experience than I am. He has certainly prepared well; his gear is brand-new and of the highest quality. If nothing else, he certainly looks the part of the intrepid African explorer.

Suddenly, out of the corner of my eye, I see him freeze. He stands, still as a statue, and then sits down heavily, the tall stalks swallowing him up from my view. I swim through the grass to where he now sits. As I come upon him, he is trembling.

"Lion" he whispers pointing to the trail behind us. I fix my gaze on where he is pointing but cannot see anything. "Lion" says Tom again, his eyes saucering.

Still unable to see anything, I try to get Tom to move, but he will not budge. He is paralyzed with fear. Leaving Tom, I rush ahead to our group and fetch Derek. He tells our guide to hold up the march and returns with me to Tom, who is still sitting where he was, shaking like a leaf.

Derek, a lifelong Outward Bound leader and executive questions Tom. "What is it? You can't sit out here in the sun all day, you know."

Derek's right. It is late afternoon; the temperature is well over 100 degrees. Even standing still, we can feel the sweat pouring off our bodies. Tom just purses his lips and stares back to the place he spotted the lion.

"Richard tells me you saw a lion. Not surprising, really." Derek brushes a clump of the tall grass with the back of his hand. "They call this stuff lion grass for a good reason."

Tom is not moved. He shakes his head and mutters something.

Derek leans closer to the sitting man. "What's that?" he asks.

Tom is silent a moment and then repeats himself. "This is insane."

"I'm not sure I'd go that far," replies Derek, assuming Tom is talking about his reaction. "But I would agree that it's not the most useful response to seeing 'Simba' in the bush."

The mention again of the lion seems to send shivers through Tom's body and loosen his tongue. "No. It's us. Here. This is crazy. Too dangerous. We shouldn't be here."

"Well, be that as it may," says Derek, "we ARE here, and there's only one way out—the way we're headed."

"I'm not going," insists Tom. "No way. No."

Tom's intransigence has brought home the reality of the African bush to not only Derek and me, but also to the rest of the group, who have filtered back and are now standing near us in various states of concern. They are wondering whether our expedition will continue.

Derek tries reasoning with Tom. "Listen, Tom, you can't just sit here. It will be getting dark soon and if we don't get to a camp near water tonight we'll all be in serious trouble tomorrow. Lions or no lions."

"I just want out of here," says Tom. "I want to go back."

Derek reminds Tom that we've already come a full day from where the truck dropped us off; besides, it is no longer there. At present, it is making its way in a big semicircle to where we plan to meet up next week. "There's nothing to go back to, Tom," says Derek, rather sternly.

"I just want out," repeats Tom. "Out of this. Right now."

Derek kneels down next to the group. He speaks to Tom, but what he says is clearly meant to be heard by all of us. "Tom, you can't get out of it. There's no getting out—this is what it is." He pauses a moment and then continues, louder, as if announcing to everyone: "We have a climbing motto at Outward Bound precisely for this sort of situation: 'If you can't get out of it, get into it!'"

Derek's words have an immediate impact on the entire group—Tom included. "If you can't get out of it, get into it!" When there is no way out of a situation, there is only one thing to do: get into it.

We realize at that point, that we are in so deep that our only recourse is to dive even deeper. Our situation is inescapable and so, instead of trying to escape it, we must embrace it. To get out of it, we have to get into it.

And so, we do.

After only a few words, the group decides to press on. We realize that heading back to where we came from is not an option; our only way out is to get into it.

Derek's advice becomes our group's mantra for the rest of the trip. We face other challenges in the week or so ahead, but with each one, we accept that the only way around it is through it. By the end of our trek, we need only give each other a look that says it all, "If you can't get out of it, get into it."

In the years since that first trip to Africa, Derek's words have come back to me time and time again. The motto never fails to create a shift in my perspective when I recall it. I have been involved in wilderness experiences—whether in the plains of Africa, the mountains of Colorado, or even the boardrooms of corporate America—and whenever I find myself or my group becoming stuck, I am reminded of this simple truth: "If you can't get out of it, get into it."

There's No Getting out of It

We recall these words now because we see so many people who are "stuck" in their "day jobs." They want out of where they are. They fantasize about winning the lottery, about becoming a millionaire, about meeting someone who will hire them and solve all their problems. In short, they fantasize about getting out of it.

But the simple fact is this: at times, there is no getting out of it. The difficulties and dissatisfactions of work can only be met in one way: head on. If we want to get out of our current situation, if we want to enjoy real joy in our work, there is only one thing to do: get into it.

How can we escape the feeling of being trapped and get into it, right where we are, in the same "day job?" Obviously, it is easier said than done. Most of us have to make a living;

consequently, we have to make compromises. We may value the natural setting of a sunny beach beside an azure sea above all else; unfortunately, though, there are only so many perfect jobs in paradise at any one time.

We can take heart from the knowledge that there are people—regular people in all walks of life—who *are* choosing to make their work, work. Their jobs are not perfect, but they are nonetheless tolerable, workable, at least from now on.

Gifts and the Good Life

One of the reasons people cite for failing to express their gifts is that they cannot make money doing so. "I've got to make a living," they'll say. "And nobody's going to pay me for doing what I love to do."

But this gives rise to an important question: Is money what it is really about, anyway?

In a classic of ancient Greek philosophy, *The Nichomachean Ethics,* Aristotle argues that the meaning of life is happiness. Everything we do, he observes, aims at some good, and all of these goods aim, in one way or another, at happiness. So, Aristotle concludes that happiness must be the highest good—in other words, the very thing that life is all about.

Aristotle's conclusion seems hard to dispute; after all, is not the pursuit of happiness the primary motivation in our lives? Is not everything we do intended—at least indirectly—to contribute to our sense of well-being and satisfaction? And, if so, what else could the meaning of life possibly be?

Of course the challenge at this point is to identify what exactly makes us happy. Aristotle surveys the usual suspects—

pleasure, honor, and money—and concludes that none of these can be the source of true happiness. Pleasure is fleeting and tends to make us feel lousy and dissipated when we overindulge. Honor is too dependent on other people; if our happiness depends primarily on what others think of us, we are going to constantly feel at the mercy of people's whims. Money is only a means to something else; moreover, it is usually the case that people undertake a life of moneymaking only because they *have* to; clearly, then, this cannot be what really makes people happy either.

Aristotle ultimately reasons that the authentically happy life is the virtuous life. The way he sees it, acting in accordance with virtue is the best expression of what it means to be human. Virtuous behavior represents human excellence in action. Since excellence is the manner in which anything best attains its ends, it follows naturally that virtuous behavior must be the manner in which human beings will best achieve happiness.

Many people today probably would not agree with Aristotle. Often, when asked what would make them happy, people say money or material goods. Just look at the success of state lotteries or get-rich-quick programs. We tell ourselves that "if only" we were rich, we would be happy. When we are dissatisfied with our jobs, we tell ourselves that money is the only reason we are staying where we are. Now, this may be. We may truly find ourselves in such a bind that we have no choice but to grin and bear it to make a living. But chances are, if we think about it more carefully, we will discover that we are not so tied down as we think we are—there are other considerations than finances that are constraining our choice.

Consider: are there certain jobs you would not do no matter how much they paid you? Imagine that you were asked to be Hitler's press agent or an executioner in a country where people were routinely put to death for simple expressions of free speech. No doubt you would refuse, no matter how large the salary.

And, it is not even necessary to take it to such extremes. We all draw the line somewhere—whether it is at engaging in selling practices we find objectionable or having to submit to regulations or policies we consider unfair or draconian.

Certainly, it is not always so easy to say, "Enough is enough;" and, of course, there is a certain amount of undesirable stuff we have to put up with in any job. It would be impractical—not to mention foolish and immature—to quit every time we felt things were not going exactly as we wished they would. Still, there is only so much any of us can take. And if we have reached that point, then we should not pretend that money is a sufficient reason for staying put. By the same token, though, if we *have not* reached that point, then we should not delude ourselves into thinking that the *only* reason we are staying where we are is the paycheck.

Reimagine Your Job

Most of us do not have the freedom to pick up and quit a job that is dissatisfying. We tend to have a good deal invested in the place we work and the people we work with. Pensions, seniority, familiarity, and more all figure into keeping us where we are—even when where we are is not where we would like to be.

So what can we do short of casting caution and good sense completely to the wind? What can we do when we are legitimately frustrated by our work situation but at the same have good reasons for not wanting to quit?

We can approach the answer to this by exploring our gifts. Examining what we consistently have the urge to give away can often help us find new ways to conceive of our jobs that lead to greater satisfaction and fulfillment.

As you think about your gifts, try to remember your first few days on at a job that really let you use them. What was it like to be doing work that enabled you to give away what your hand naturally turns to? How does that compare with where you are now? A job is like a love affair in some ways. As we become more familiar with it, we tend to overlook things—often the very things that drew us to it in the first place.

It can be helpful, therefore, to reacquaint ourselves with our jobs. By reimagining our work with a fresh outlook, we can uncover opportunities for utilizing our gifts we may not have recognized. By looking at our jobs with a new—that is, old—perspective, we can sometimes discover unseen—or merely forgotten—pathways to where we would like to be.

This exercise, then, is quite simple. All it asks you to do is come to work with the perspective you had the first day on the job. Imagine that it is all new. Imagine that you have not experienced the various events that affect your current attitudes about the things you do. Imagine you are sitting at your desk for the first time and that all the tasks you have to accomplish are the very first assignments you are undertaking on the job.

Now ask yourself: what really attracts my energy? Which of the things I am doing do I especially enjoy? Which of my many responsibilities provides me the fullest opportunity for expressing who I really am?

Your answers may surprise you. You may discover that you have forgotten how much you enjoy some things that may have become routine. By the same token, you may be reminded that some of what you do most is what you like least. It may be that you have fallen into habits that are just habitual. You may be doing things not because they in any way express your calling, but just because you are doing them.

Now, admittedly, some of this is likely to be beyond your control. No doubt some of your job responsibilities are requirements whether you want them to be or not. However, it is also likely that some potential dissatisfactions you may be experiencing are responsibilities you do not have to shoulder. You may be putting yourself in a situation you do not really need to be in. You may be bearing a burden that is not necessary.

No Whiners Allowed

There is no comparing suffering. A doctor who is unhappy in her job—even though she makes a good living and has a loving family—clearly is not in as dire straits as someone who is out of work and all alone in the world. But it would be unfair to say that the doctor has no reason to complain. Our feelings are, of course, based on our experience of the world, but it is *our experience.* If the doctor in this case finds her work meaningless or deeply at odds with what she truly cares about, then it is perfectly understandable that she could be unhappy. No one should say that just because there are other people who live lives that, externally, are much more difficult, the doctor is not justified in feeling the way she does.

On the other hand, those of us who enjoy certain privileges—even the relatively minor privilege of being able to read a book like this and think about issues such as calling—need to admit that we have more abundant options for doing something about undesirable situations in which we find ourselves. In contemporary society, people with skills and education have a greater degree of flexibility and freedom in their choices of career than ever before. If we find ourselves complaining that we are hopelessly stuck in our job, then we probably have not fully explored one of two options. Either we have not examined all the possibilities for change within our job, or we have not looked carefully enough at what is more broadly available.

Mattering Matters

A common theme among people who are fulfilled in their work is that they see the big picture. They recognize that the work they are doing can make a positive difference in the world—even if it is just a small difference. What matters to them is that their work matters. And it matters because it improves—not just their own life but also, more importantly, someone else's life.

People like this value what they do because they conceive of what they do as a choice. They implicitly ask, "What gift do I bring to the world?" And they answer in a way that enables them to express their deepest values through an expression of their gifts right here, right now. They reimagine real possibilities, in part, because they have come to develop a sense of perspective on what really matters and how much is enough.

How Much *Is* Enough?

In order to successfully reimagine work, we must ask ourselves the question, "How much do I need?" Although we may be inclined to answer, "As much as I can get!," we have to be honest: this does not escape the question; it only kicks the can a bit further down the road. One approach, therefore, is to break the "enoughness" inquiry down into three component parts:

- What is my calling?

- What (apart from money) keeps me from living my calling?

- What role would "enough" money play in helping me to live my calling?

By highlighting money in the equation, we can better see its role; we can begin to clarify what it is actually needed for and how much of it is "enough."

Developing a good relationship with money involves mediating the tension between concerns over finances and hopes for one's life. Given the central role that money plays in our day-to-day existence, it naturally follows that it is a source of much worry. There is nothing unnatural about that; it would be unrealistic to expect a complete lack of anxiety about our bank accounts and nest eggs. Worry about such things is part of life. But the goal of the reimagined life, one might say, is to worry well. To "worry well" about money means clarifying why and how we should care about it.

The key to this is self-awareness. Self-awareness—the true antidote to worry—does not make legitimate financial troubles go away. Rather, it enables us to live in accordance with calling in spite of our concerns about money.

Reimagining requires that we look closely at our relationship with money. It is not about minimizing the vital role it plays in our lives; rather, we seek to develop a wise relationship with money; we seek to worry well about it. In doing so, we bring imagination and our own ideas about the good life into the mix.

"Enough" for the Good Life

Unless we are Donald Duck's uncle, Scrooge McDuck, who likes nothing more than to bathe himself in the stacks of gold coins he has amassed, we will have to admit to ourselves that money is mainly a means to an end. Yet surprisingly, people often confuse the end they are seeking—the good life—with the means to it—money.

This is in no way meant to imply that trying to make a good living to live a good life is wrong; far from it. Financial security can liberate us from having to do things we find meaningless just to make ends meet. Moreover, nearly everyone wants nice things, and money can help add beauty, stability, and comfort to our lives. We need money to survive and we seek money, so we can buy things that we think will make us happy: cars, clothes, homes, holidays, etcetera.

But there is plenty of research suggesting that money provides a diminishing return in terms of happiness. Levels of happiness tend to rise rather quickly as people move from having no money to modest amounts of it; then the increase levels off. The measured happiness of people making median incomes is not significantly different than for those at the very highest income levels.

Nobel prize winning economist Daniel Kahneman found little correlation between riches and positive emotions. He reports, "the belief that high income is associated with good mood is widespread, but mostly illusory. People with above-average income are relatively satisfied with their lives but are barely happier than others in moment-to-moment experience."

Perhaps this should not surprise us. When we talk about happiness—the good life—what do we have in mind? If it is something like "living in the right place, with people we love, doing the right work, on purpose," then it is clear that the role of money is important but not all there is to it.

"Is This All There Is?"

With money, we can indeed buy things that may help us feel secure. But the most important components of the good life have no fixed relationship with a hefty bank account. There is certainly no shortage of people with lots of nice things who feel bored, sad, and depressed. In fact, any number of popular reality TV programs are built around just this premise! And as it turns out, a good percentage of people feel worse once they have attained material success. Having been stripped of the illusion that money can buy happiness, they are left wondering "What now?" and "Is this all there is?" This is the awful truth they must face: money can buy the symbols of happiness, but it cannot purchase the source.

That source, as most of us know in our hearts, is a life of meaning and purpose, in which we do things for other people, and make a real difference in the lives of those we care about. It is most often the invisible, not the visible, that bring us meaning and happiness. True happiness requires getting on with the things that are important to us, expressing our gifts, actively trying to realize what we care about and bring it into life. But these activities are more complicated than just going out shopping.

A good life is still a life. Inevitably it will include its full share of pain, loneliness, disappointment, and loss. To live a life that is good involves all of this.

Reimagining captures what people actually aspire to—the best use of our gifts, involvement in things we care about, the formation and expression of our values, and the emergence of our best selves. That is why "the good life" is a more accurate term than happiness for what we really want in life.

So, if it is true that more money does not result in more happiness, then seeking more and more money as a means to more happiness hardly seems like the best way to go about it. Insofar as we make choices that focus more on the material than on the emotional, we are going astray. Laurence Boldt says in *Zen and the Art of Making a Living,* "Society tells us the only things that matter is matter; the only things that count are the things that can be counted." Could this be, as Boldt implies, another bit of bad advice on the part of society-at-large?

The problem, of course, is that we all need a sufficient store of money in order to live. There may not be all that much we can accomplish emotionally with lots of money, but there are certainly innumerable things we cannot accomplish practically without it. The wise poet, philosopher, and farmer Wendell Berry, writes in his well-known essay "Solving For Pattern," that "A good solution always answers the question, 'How much is enough?'" While the answer may not always be clear, it is clear that the answer is not always "more."

Can Money Buy Happiness?

Reimagining shifts perspective from a focus on money to a focus on the good life, recognizing that happiness is the ultimate currency, the end towards which all others converge. Aristotle made this explicit when he said, "happiness is the meaning and the purpose of life, the whole aim and end of human existence."

The Dalai Lama claims that "whether one believes in religion or not; whether one believes in this religion or that religion, the very purpose of our life is happiness, the very motion of our life is towards happiness."

The currency through which we reimagine our work and our lives—our perceptions of what matters—has wide-reaching consequences, for ourselves and for society as a whole. We enjoy higher levels of happiness and society runs more smoothly when we accept the reality that happiness is the ultimate currency.

Living a good life requires asking and answering that perennial and difficult question: "How much is enough?" It involves finding the overlap between that question and the even broader one: "What is my calling?"

If we get stuck in the mode of trying to buy happiness with money, then our satisfaction at work is anchored to our paycheck. But once we break our emotional connection between money and the good life, a whole new realm of possibilities is opened upon and we are able to bring our best to all our work, including what we do for income. No longer are we expecting our paid position to fulfill our need for meaning, as well. Now we can clearly determine how much it is worth relative to our real purpose. We may choose to reduce the amount of time we work for money or change jobs to pursue more of what gives meaning to our lives.

How Much Do You Make?

Ask nearly anyone, "How much do you make?" and you will have entered extremely secret and deeply emotional territory. Philosopher Jacob Needleman says, "Money has become for our generation what sex was for earlier generations—a force that is at the back of almost everything people do, which we're not yet able to face without hypocrisy." Yet, if we are committed to finding fulfilling work, we must confront that force, and face the hypocrisy, by clearly identifying the role money plays in our life.

Many people feel that work is a burden and pursue money in the belief that when they are rich enough, they will have the freedom to follow their dreams. It rarely works that way, though. By analogy, Dave remembers when, as a teenager, he was trying to learn bass guitar. "I can't wait until I'm good," he said, "then I'll have fun playing it." His friend, Paul, wisely pointed out that if he did not enjoy the instrument now, it was unlikely he would ever enjoy it. Dave saw his point, took up the flute instead, which he loved practicing right from the start. The same idea goes for deferred enjoyment in life. Doing something in order to earn to the money to do what you really want to do can become an endless merry-go-round.

The work of purpose must be ever present within us, and we need to act on our passion each and every day.

True wealth is having enough for our needs and finding satisfaction with what we have as opposed to what we do not. Such riches come from deep awareness of and connection to our calling. When the questions that guide us are more about finding greater meaning than acquiring more money, we are much more likely to derive satisfaction from the journey as opposed to the destination. When our work and life are based on what is inside rather than outside, then whatever we have will be enough.

What Is Success?

Success is: _____.

How would you fill in the blank? There is certainly no shortage of answers out there. Walk into any bookstore, peruse myriad websites, talk to countless experts, and you will learn "How to Be Successful," where "success" inevitably means being rich (and probably famous too). More often than not, success correlates to money, possessions, power, and recognition.

Next time you go to a high school or college reunion, pay special attention to the main topics of conversation. Other than who got fat, who got divorced, or who died, it is all about who turned out to be really successful—in other words, who made the most money.

Popular culture would have us believe that success is all about money, power, and pleasure, but the numerous stories of unfulfilled lives and burnout among the so-called successful suggest that real success may be something different altogether.

For confirmation, we need only refer back to our old friend, Aristotle. Writing nearly 2,500 years ago, he pointed out that most people are mistaken in their conception of the good life. Neither money, nor fame, nor pleasure will suffice in the long run, as all are fleeting in their own way. Something else is required and it involves a life of excellence in conjunction with virtue—in short a life of meaning and purpose.

Be a Success or Live a Successful Life?

Arianna Huffington provides a telling example in her book, *Thrive.* In 2007, she was on top of the world. Wealthy and celebrated as one of the world's most influential women, she was a cover story example of what it usually means to be a success. As cofounder and editor-in-chief of the Huffington Post, she was a name brand recognized around the globe.

However, in April of that year, Arianna collapsed from exhaustion and hit her head on her desk. She spent the next months going from doctor to doctor trying to figure out what was wrong, all the while wondering whether this was really what success looked like. In her own words: "In terms of the traditional measure of success, which focuses on money and power, I was very successful. But I was not living a successful life by any sane definition of success."

As Arianna eventually figured out, living a successful life involves more than money or fame. Above all, it has to do with the manner in which we conduct our lives and the connections we make with others. There are plenty of people who have millions of dollars but not a single true friend. Would you consider them a success? More importantly, what would they say? In an ideal world, this dichotomy between human connection and financial achievement would not exist; we would all have lots of friends and lots of money. So why is it that the most widely accepted idea of success revolves around money?

Is it possible to be "successful" while still being a "successful human being?" Of course, but it is difficult. Accumulating material wealth takes time—time which usually limits the amount of attention one can spend on fostering meaningful relationships. But by focusing on one's calling and using that focus to make clear choices about what to say "yes" to and what to say "no" to, it is possible to make a good living while at the same time, making a good life.

The Process Works if You Work the Process

Richard has long made a claim about exercises and activities designed to help us identify our calling or simply achieve a consistent level of satisfaction in some aspect of our daily lives. The key to success is a willingness to commit consistently to the process and see where it leads. It is easy for us to get sidetracked by self-doubt or confusion or just plain laziness. On the other hand, if we are willing to take the necessary steps to keep moving forward, we will eventually arrive at our hoped-for (but perhaps unexpected) destination.

His "mantra" for this attitude is, "The process works if you work the process." And, while literally thousands of people who have participated in events he has led can attest to the truth of this claim in those contexts, it is also the case that working the process works in other areas of our lives, as well.

The tradition of "practice" is an ancient and venerable one. In the Buddhist tradition, for instance, the practice of silent meditation is a core discipline. In Hinduism, the Vedic tradition, we find the physical practice of yoga asana or posture practice. More familiar to those of us in the West, there is the practice of prayer in the Judeo-Christian-Islamic, or Abrahamic tradition. While the particulars of these various schools of thought or ways of being may differ, they all share a common insight about the importance of having a regular practice.

Point being: as Richard would put it, "The process works if you work the process."

How then, does this relate to the topic of this chapter—"Should you quit your day job? To begin with, it is useful to recognize that the effort to hear and uncover one's calling is an ongoing process. It is a practice. And to achieve success in that practice, a steady, ongoing commitment to it is key.

Secondly, we may also benefit from reminding ourselves that we learn just as much—if not more—from failure than we do from success. Mistakes are the most powerful tools for learning available to us. When we try something out, and it does not go as planned, we increase our knowledge. By contrast, what typically gets in the way of our personal growth and development is a resistance to taking chances. Too often, we are motivated—or more precisely, de-motivated—by a fear of what might go wrong. This tends to make us less likely to the do very things we need to do to have things come out right. The takeaway from this, then, is that it is worthwhile to engage in one's practice even if prospects for success are cloudy. While we may not always succeed when we make an effort, it is certain that we do not if we do not.

CHAPTER 3

Reimagining Gifts—
How Do You Do It?

The Napkin Test

When people meet Richard and find out that he is a life coach, they invariably ask him, "Say, do you have a minute? Could you tell me what to do for the rest of my life?" In response to this inquiry, he has them do what we call "The Napkin Test." You can try it right now, yourself.

Grab your typical cocktail napkin (or similarly-sized piece of paper.) On it, write down the following simple formula: G + P + V = C, where "G" stands for Gifts, "P" stands for "Passion," "V" stands for "Values," and "C" stands for Calling.

Gifts + Passions + Values = Calling. It is really that simple. Uncovering our calling means identifying our gifts, applying them in support of something we are passionate about, in an environment that is consistent with our values. That, in essence, is what reimagining work is all about.

Did You Choose Your Work or Did Your Work Choose You?

Very few people have always known what they wanted to be. Sure, you hear stories about artists or writers who, upon first picking up paintbrush or pen, never looked back. Picasso, for instance, began drawing seriously at age ten and was already exhibiting in galleries by the time he was thirteen. For most of us, though, the realization of what we were meant to do is quite elusive. Few young people stop to think about what their life's work is—and even among those who do, rare is the belief that they can make a living at it.

So most of us essentially drift into our occupations. Our lives unfold in a certain manner, and as they do, we make choices from those that are presented to us. There is nothing wrong with this, and some of us are lucky enough to fall into the perfect thing via this process, but it is pretty obvious that this is not the best way to hear and heed our life's calling.

It is also obvious that many of us *fail* to discover our calling in this haphazard way. When we do, we find ourselves at some point in our lives—usually around mid-life—asking ourselves the *big* questions. Questions like: "Who am I?" "What was I really meant to do?" "What would truly make me happy?"

That sense of being disconnected from our authentic self is pervasive. It is why so many people feel so lost. Sidetracked. Stuck. We wonder if we can possibly change course and find our way back to the person we really are.

How do we choose work that expresses our calling?

The answer lies in the exploration we undertake with the Napkin Test: our gifts, passions, and values. A good job, career, or calling blends all three together.

Reimagining Gifts

Our *gifts* are those special aptitudes that we were born with. They are the force behind those things we love to do and do well, and that we never needed to learn. Our gifts are innate, but we naturally feel compelled to give them away; we simply enjoy the doing itself. We feel our gifts deeply, in the marrow of our bones.

Expressing our gifts is what we do naturally, effortlessly, and without regard for what we might receive in return. Gifts are deeper aptitudes than talents. Take, for example, a phenomenally gifted businessperson like the late Steve Jobs. His special ability was inspiring people to organize themselves around a vision for the future. Many individual skills and talents go into this; he was obviously an excellent speaker, creator, product designer, and so on. But his gift, and the gift of others who are similarly successful in galvanizing support for visionary efforts, was greater than the sum of these parts.

When we explore our own gifts, therefore, we want to think in deep terms. We want to look beneath our talents to what motivates them. We want to explore what we are consistently and enjoyably giving to others.

There is a natural connection between our gifts and the most fulfilling aspects of our jobs. So, one way to get at the nature of our gifts is to ask ourselves the following question: *What gift was I expressing the last time I was so absorbed that I lost all track of time?*

When we are expressing our gifts, we tend to get into what Mihaly Csikszentmihalyi, in his book *Flow: The Psychology of Optimal Experience* calls a state of "flow." We become so deeply involved in what we are doing, that the clock seems to melt away. Time becomes irrelevant. An hour, even an entire day can go by in a single instant. We are so absorbed in the moment that the moments fly by.

Think about the last time you experienced this sense of flow. What were you doing? More importantly, *what was it about* what you were doing that made it so fulfilling? You might, for instance, have been making a presentation to team members or clients. *What was it about* presenting that turned you on? Communicating? Motivating? Selling? Look behind the presentation itself to discover what your gifts are. Then notice that expressing these gifts forms a common thread in the activities that really move you—your Calling Card.

It is also quite illuminating to wonder how your natural gifts were or were not encouraged. The lucky ones among us tended to have our gifts nurtured by parents, schoolteachers, and colleagues. Many people though, have had to really fight to express their gifts—and, for many, the struggle has proven too much. Rather than find ways to make their gifts come alive, they have chosen to let what is natural lie dormant. While this is quite practical, it is deeply unfortunate. Our gifts continually *seek* expression; a life lived without allowing our gifts to flourish is a life less than fully lived.

It is never too late, though, to uncover and revitalize our gifts, and by working with our Calling Card to do this, we continue the ongoing process of reimagining work.

Reimagining Passions

What are you curious about? What issues or causes really move you? What problems in the world or work world do you think need solving? When you lie awake at night obsessing over the state of the universe, what obsesses you most? In the answers to questions like these we discover our passions. Our passions are the issues we care most deeply about. When we connect our gifts to our passions, we have a clear reason to get up in the morning. Passions are what inspire us; they are, in artistic terms, our muses, the force that inspires us. When we are passionate about something—a cause, an endeavor, a project that speaks to us—we are driven to devote time and energy to it. We become creative in unexpected and unprecedented ways.

Passions can take many forms. They can be quite specific: you may be passionate, for instance, about bicycles. You may feel that the bicycle represents the savior of humanity and may spend a good deal of your free time working on bicycle-related causes. Passions may also be rather broad: you may be passionate, for instance, about the environment. You may feel deeply committed to expanding people's environmental awareness. You may spend your free time devoted to causes that seek to create a more just and sustainable world. Passions may be somewhere in the middle, too: you may be passionate, for instance, about community. You may spend your free time working to strengthen the connections between people in your neighborhood or town. You may be drawn to any number of organizations or activities that share this driving passion of yours.

What is important to realize about passions is that they are only passions if they are "alive." That is, they only count as passions if we feel them deeply. This does not mean we have to monopolize the conversation whenever their subject comes up; it does mean, however, that we have to feel strongly about them and have an inclination—realized or not—to act in their support. It does not make sense to say, "Oh, one of my passions is the environment, but I don't feel any desire to do anything about it." Our passions have to move us or else they are not really passions. Moreover, they must ignite us consistently; passions run as an undercurrent throughout our lives.

So, to get a better sense of your own passions, ask yourself: *What keeps me up at night? What do I think is worth doing with my time? What do I obsess about? What challenges do I think need solving? What am I constantly reading about and talking to people about?*

The common themes that emerge from this inquiry will give you a better sense of what your passions really are.

Reimagining Values

What environments are best for you to work in? How do you prefer to operate in the world of work? What type of work culture best suits your style?

Answers to these questions point you in the direction of your values. Values are the expression of our deepest beliefs. They are the markers that guide our gifts and passions. As such, they determine in what environments we are likely to be most successful and fulfilled.

When we are working in environments that are consistent with our core values, we feel energized and enthusiastic about what we are doing; we cannot wait to get up and go to work.

It is important to keep in mind that values are active; valuing is something we *do*. If one of your values is, say, fairness, then that means you consistently make it a point to treat your colleagues equitably. This care consistently colors everything you do. Values are only values *because* they are acted upon. If we stop acting on something, then it no longer counts as a value. If you do not regularly make an effort to see that people get what they deserve and deserve what they get, then it is inaccurate to say that you value fairness.

Our values are expressed through the work that we do and the manner in which we do it. Notice again the *active* aspect of values.

What is important to keep in mind about values is that they—more than any of the other components of calling—expose our individuality. Our values reflect the characteristic way we express ourselves; consequently, two people may have very similar gifts, and passions but still have quite different values.

Labor of Love

A calling is not something you do to impress other people or to get rich quick. It is a labor of love that is intrinsically satisfying. It is something you would happily do even if it never makes you rich or famous. Of course, there is nothing wrong with making money or being widely-acclaimed, but we should also recognize that there are other ways to pursue a calling: helping others, learning, promoting change, or dedicating oneself to an art form.

Our callings are made manifest in our choices and in the unpredictable and serendipitous events that take place in our lives. Unless we bring our calling to light, though, it remains hidden from the world. Our calling is invisible except in action.

Uncovering our calling, though, can be made easier through the use of the Calling Cards—a list of natural preferences that have emerged in our discussions and research with hundreds of people over the last few decades.

The Purpose of Calling Cards

Historically, calling cards, also known as visiting cards, were small paper cards with one's name printed on it, often along with an artistic design of some kind. They were used in the eighteenth and nineteenth centuries as a way for people to introduce themselves to others. Etiquette required that you should not expect to visit someone else at home without first leaving your calling card. Upon leaving your card, you would not be admitted at first, but might receive a card at your own home in response. This would serve as a signal that a personal visit and meeting at home would be welcome. On the other hand, if no card was forthcoming, or a card was sent in an envelope, a personal visit was thereby discouraged.

The Calling Cards, as we use them here, are a tool for you to introduce yourself to yourself. They are a way for you to call on yourself, via a clarification of your true gifts. Your Calling Card, the one you choose through the calling cards process, provides insight into *who you are.* Consider it the next step in the advancement of Calling Card protocol.

Imagine that you have your calling printed on the back of your business card. The front side, as usual, displays your title—what you do. But the back displays your Calling Card—who you are. In this way, your business card now communicates *both* your form and your essence. Your title is the form of your work—it is what you do. Your calling is the essence of your work—it is who you are.

If you were to change jobs, the front of your business card would change; you'd get a new title. But the back of your card—your essence—would remain the same. Calling is something you bring to your work; it stays with you wherever you go.

Each of the callings describes a core gift. Each calling comes directly out of someone's experience. We have been collecting callings in seminars, workshops, and coaching sessions with individuals and groups from all walks of life. The list of fifty-two callings we have come up with represents the "essence of essences" in our research. (This does not mean that there are not other callings than our fifty-two; it does, however, mean that these fifty-two represent those that have best withstood real-world testing.)

Using the Calling Cards in a simple self-examination helps us name our calling—that gift which is invisible but wants to be unwrapped and given away.

The Power of Words

The lives we live emerge from the words we choose to define our lives.

The descriptors on the Calling Cards are deliberately open to interpretation. And to some extent, choosing one over another is equally subjective. But importantly, it is a matter of choice. Choosing a particular card, identifying with it—even if that identification feels somewhat arbitrary—is a way of naming something powerful that emanates from within. Doing so allows us to understand ourselves better via the words we have selected on our own.

REALISTIC

Building Things
Fixing Things
Growing Things
Making Things Work
Shaping Environments
Solving Problems
Moving Things Physically

ENTERPRISING

Making Deals
Selling Intangibles
Exploring the Way
Persuading People
Opening Doors
Empowering Others
Starting Things
Bringing Out Potential
Managing Things

ARTISTIC

Adding Humor
Breaking Molds
Creating Things
Composing Themes
Designing Things
Performing Events
Seeing Possibilities
Seeing the Big Picture
Writing Things

STRUCTURED

Organizing Things
Doing the Numbers
Processing Things
Operating Things
Getting Things Right
Straightening Things Up

SOCIAL

Awakening Spirit
Bringing Joy
Building Relationships
Creating Dialogue
Facilitating Change
Getting Participation
Healing Wounds
Helping Overcome Obstacles
Instructing People
Resolving Disputes
Creating Trust
Giving Care

INVESTIGATIVE

Advancing Ideas
Analyzing Information
Discovering Resources
Investigating Things
Getting to the Heart
of Matters
Making Connections
Putting the Pieces Together
Researching Things
Translating Things

So, as you examine the Calling Cards, listen carefully to what you are telling yourself. To find fulfillment in our work, we need a clear, simple way to name our gifts. We need to reframe our concept of calling until the words feel natural and come to us easily. We must settle for nothing less than a description of calling that fits us and no one else exactly the same way. No one can choose our calling for us; no one else can tell us how to express our calling once it is found. Each of us, individually, must hear and heed our role in the world. Each of us must choose or create the Calling Card that expresses the gifts we feel an inner urge to give away.

So... go within. Examine the Calling Cards. Explore the possibilities of calling. Name your calling.

The Calling Cards

Here is the list of Calling Cards. Following this are instructions for using them. You may also find it useful to complete the online version of this Calling Cards activity (and many others) after signing up for free at the Life Reimagined website at: https://lifereimagined.aarp.org/. A direct link to the Calling Cards is: http://lifereimagined.org/activity/calling-cards.

List of Calling Cards

Advancing Ideas

Adding Humor

Awakening Spirit

Breaking Molds

Bringing Joy

Building Things

Creating Dialogue

Organizing Things

Researching Things

Designing Things

Discovering Resources

Creating Trust

Seeing Possibilities	Moving Physically
Persuading People	Shaping Environments
Exploring the Way	Instructing People
Facilitating Change	Managing Things
Composing Themes	Writing Things
Fixing Things	Processing Things
Getting Things Right	Translating Things
Getting to the Heart of Matters	Empowering Others
Helping Overcome Obstacles	Doing the Numbers
Building Relationships	Straightening Things Up
Investigating Things	Growing Things
Giving Care	Analyzing Information
Making Connections	Starting Things
Making Things Work	Creating Things
Opening Doors	Healing Wounds
Putting the Pieces Together	Making Deals
Operating Things	Solving Problems
Seeing the Big Picture	Resolving Disputes
Bringing Out Potential	Getting Participation
Selling Intangibles	Performing Events

Calling Cards Instructions

Step 1: Your Natural Preferences

Examine the entire list of fifty-two callings. As you study them, arrange the callings in three groups according to your natural preferences.

Group #1: Those that fit your gifts.

Group #2: Not sure if they fit your gifts.

Group #3: Those that do not feel like your gifts at all. Do not rush. Use your intuition. What does your hand turn to naturally? What calls to you? Continue to look through the first two groups to identify those callings that fit you best.

Ask yourself: What do I love to do? For each selection, think of an example of a time you expressed that gift.

Step 2: Your Five Most Natural Preferences

Concentrate on the Group #1 callings. Explore them more carefully. Which ones seem to be the "best of the best?" Without thinking too much about it, identify the ones that seem to call to you automatically. Select the top five callings from this group—those that best describe what you naturally love doing.

Ask yourself again: What do I most love to do?

Step 3: Your Single Most Natural Preference

Consider the five callings you have selected. Knowing yourself as you do, which one card seems to "call to you"? Which is the one that, today, feels most consistent with what you love to do? If you were forced to pick just one, which one would it be?

Ask yourself: Does this truly give me joy in the actual doing of it? What are some examples?

An alternative way to arrive at Your Single Most Natural Preference is to work through the callings, pairing them two-by-two, and choosing which of the pair you think more accurately reflects your calling. This works especially well with a partner.

Set the callings down between you and your partner. Have your partner name the first two callings quickly —within three seconds or so—choose which is a better expression of your calling. Put the "winner" in one group, set the "loser" aside. (If you honestly cannot decide—that is, if they are both "winners," put them both in the "winning" group. If neither seems appropriate for you at all, discard them both.)

Having gone through the callings once, you will have a group of twenty-six winners. Repeat the process from above, going through all twenty-six. Now you will have thirteen winners. Repeat the process with this group. You will have six winners. Then three. Then one. This final "winning" card is your Calling Card.

And again, we encourage you to try the online version of this Calling Card exercise.

Step 4: Your Calling Card

Study your number one card. If the words do not fit exactly, feel free to edit so your own calling describes you accurately. You may find it useful to use words from your top five callings to enhance your number one card.

Step 5: Make a Call

Discuss your Calling Card with a close friend or family member. See if others have insight into your calling that can help you refine it further.

Step 6: Imagine a Call

Imagine that you could do any kind of work in the world, anything at all—as long as it fits your Calling Card. Jot down three or four things you can see yourself doing. What does this list tell you about your calling?

Step 7: Heed the Call

Perhaps you're thinking: "This Calling Card looks great. But it's not my day job! Moreover, I don't have the financial resources or personal freedom to do the work I love the most. How do I heed the call when I first have to heed my bills?" If you're asking questions like that, ask yourself these questions instead:

- Does your work give you a small opportunity—like the taxi driver in the earlier chapter—to express your calling? Does it ever let you do what you most enjoy doing?

- While you are working, do you ever get the sense that you are in the right place doing the right thing? How often does it happen? When it happens, what are you doing?

- What is one thing—a little thing—you could do right now to express your calling at work? What is stopping you?

It's Not What You Do, It's How You Do It

Having chosen our Calling Card, we are faced with the un-

avoidable choice of whether to answer that call. Either we do
or we do not—and the time to decide has arrived.

Any kind of work can provide us with opportunities for expressing our calling. Calling is not our job, it is what we *bring
to* our job. The core idea of calling is a simple and liberating
truth: "It is not what you do that matters, it is how you do it."
That is why we emphasize over and over the idea of "uncovering" our calling. Calling is there, all the time, just waiting to be
revealed. The choices we make allow our calling to shine forth.

In order to understand this aspect of calling more fully,
it is helpful to ask yourself two questions. The first is *"What
do you do?"* What kind of work are you currently performing?
How aligned is it with your naturally enjoyed gifts? Should you
stay or leave your current job? The second question is *"How do
you do it?"* What part of your job fulfills your sense of calling?
How can you give away your gifts even if you are in a job that
is not exactly what you want to be doing? How can you express
your calling, even if it is only partially?

Elements of our calling can be expressed in almost any job.
When we begin to see what we do as an opportunity for heeding our calling, nothing changes—but everything changes. We
still have our cab to drive, our patients to care for, our clients to
serve. We still have our up days and down days, empowering
colleagues and irritating colleagues, interesting projects and
boring projects. We still have days when it is hard to get out of
bed in the morning. Nothing seems to have changed.

On the other hand, everything has changed. By expressing
our calling, even in small, partial ways, our work is suddenly
more fulfilling. We find meaning in what we do, even when it
is not exactly what we were meant to be doing. On occasion,

throughout the workday, we feel that we are in the right place, with the right people, doing the right work, on purpose.

When this happens, even for an instant, we experience who we are and what we do as one. We experience the power of heeding our calling, the feeling of aliveness that comes from giving our gifts away to someone who needs them, in order to create something that would not have existed without us. It is the fulfilling feeling that heeding our calling means to make common: the feeling of whistling while we work!

Where Did My Gifts Come From?

Once again, we define calling as "the inner urge to give our gifts away." So, the important thing to remember about our gifts is that they are just that: *gifts.*

The perennial "nature vs. nurture" question inevitably arises here. Are born with our gifts or did we acquire them? This debate is intractable. Our answer, therefore, is both. We were born with natural preferences—some obvious, some hidden. It seems most likely that our gifts are both inborn and developed. Consider people you know who are accomplished musicians. Chances are they felt some kind of kinship with their instrument the first time they played it, but they also invested a lot of hard work to get good at it.

The "nature vs. nurture" question often comes up for Dave's students when they play the game described earlier, "Hand Dealt." They typically puzzle over the idea of what it means to be "dealt a hand" that includes certain strengths and weaknesses. Why does that happen? Who is dealing the hand? One response they sometimes explore together comes from the Indian philosopher, Sarvepalli Radhakrishnan who takes on the question in light of the traditional conception of karma. Radhakrishnan actually uses the metaphor of cards being dealt. He proposes that karma, understood simply as cause and effect, "deals" us a hand at birth, but then, it is up to each of to play that hand to the best of our abilities and in conjunction with opportunities that present themselves. Perhaps this is one way to think about our gifts and where they come from.

All of us have gifts; oddly, though, many of us have a difficult time identifying them. Ironically, the things we are best at are those that are most difficult for us to see. Most people can quite readily identify their weaknesses. Far fewer of us can say with assurance what our strengths are.

Part of this is because our gifts are things we perform with ease; generally, we have not had to work to receive our gifts, so we are apt to overlook them. More importantly, since our gifts have come to us so easily, we tend to devalue them. All our lives we are told that only things that require hard work are valuable; since our gifts are things we do relatively effortlessly, they must not be worth much.

Identifying our gifts, therefore, can be difficult. (It is hard, after all, to identify something that we cannot see and that we think is hardly worth anything.) So, one of the most effective ways to pick them out is to ask friends, family members, and colleagues. The people in our life often have a better handle on our gifts than we do. People who know us well can usually say quite easily what we do well. They recognize our gifts in action in ways that we do not. This is obvious if we think about our own friends and family; we often marvel at their abilities—feel jealous even—while they take them totally for granted. You probably have friends who can fix anything, or who are fantastic chefs, or who always seems to know the right thing to say to make someone feel better. But if you tell them about how impressed you are with what they can do, they will just shrug their shoulders and say it is no big deal. And as a matter of fact, they will probably go on to point out one of *your* gifts that they are impressed by. So it works both ways—and ends up providing you with an opportunity for getting to know your own gifts a little better.

Another way to identify our gifts is to work backwards from our Calling Card. Since we express our calling when we are using our gifts to do work we are passionate about in an environment that is consistent with our values, we might recall times that we felt particularly in touch with our calling. For example, if we remember Dave's calling—*creating dialogue*—and his classroom experience of expressing his calling, some of his gifts will become apparent, notably facilitating discussions, listening actively, and, in general, teaching.

So go back to your own Calling Card. Reflect upon an occasion—in either your personal or professional life—when you were particularly engaged. What were you doing? Were you in a "flow" state? Which of your gifts were you expressing? If the answer remains unclear, you might try writing a paragraph or two about the experience. Then share what you have written with a friend. Between the two of you, a fresh perspective on your gifts will emerge.

CHAPTER 4

Reimagining Passions—
Why Do You Do It?

What *IS* Work, Anyway?

To explore the nature of meaningful work, we must confront the *big* philosophical question: "What is the meaning of life?" In *The Meaning of Life*, philosopher Hugh S. Moorhead collected statements on life's meaning from 250 writers and scholars. Novelist James Michener wrote: "The main purpose of life is: 1) to have a job in whose purpose you can believe; 2) to have friends whose immediate purposes you can trust; 3) to have some spot on earth which you can return to as home; and 4) to be at the same time a citizen of the world."

It is no surprise that Michener lists work first.

"We put our love where we have put our labor," wrote Emerson. "To work is to pray," said St. Benedict. "Far and away the best prize that life offers is the chance to work hard at work worth doing," said Theodore Roosevelt. Love, prayer, a prize—is this how you see work? And if you do not, is it not a shame? Is there not something missing when we spend most of our lives, and certainly the greater part of our waking hours, engaged in something that is not a gesture of love, a prayer, or a prize? Faulkner wrote that one of the saddest things is that the only thing people can do for eight hours a day, day after, day, is work. He observed that we cannot eat or drink or make love for eight hours—and literally, he is right. But when our work sustains us, when it becomes an act of love, then perhaps it is not so sad at all. Perhaps it is something to celebrate. Perhaps eight hours a day is not even long enough to really sustain things.

Unfortunately, it is difficult to hold this attitude when we feel like what we are doing is not connected to our most enjoyed gifts. Work becomes drudgery, or worse, when all we are doing is putting in our time to make money. Far from being love or prayer or a prize, our job seems like a forced march through a desolate and unforgiving landscape.

Finding the natural satisfaction that our work potentially affords us involves, as we have seen, fully utilizing our natural gifts to support something we really care about. What is important to remember, though, is that this "something" does not have to be a matter of saving the world. It can be something much smaller, as long as the role it plays in our own lives is sufficiently large. It does not even have to involve the best aspects of people's lives; a perfectly satisfying—and meaningful—life can be derived from dealing on a daily basis with what most people choose not to deal with.

Life as a Set of Possibilities

If you were just going on appearances, you would probably be surprised to discover that Bill Strickland is a true visionary. A plainspoken middle-aged man with gentle eyes, he seems more like a high school science teacher than someone who is absolutely serious about changing the world in his lifetime. But this would be just the first of many ways that Bill would surprise you. You would also be surprised by his story: how an inner-city kid from one of Pittsburgh's worst neighborhoods found direction in his life through ceramic arts and ended up as executive director of two world-class organizations—the Bidwell Training Center and the Manchester Craftsmen's Guild (MCG)—which provide vocational, technical, and arts education to young people and adults from throughout western Pennsylvania. You would shake your head in wonder to find out he was able to convince the Carnegie Foundation to finance the construction of Bidwell's warm and welcoming campus building—designed by Frank Lloyd Wright's protégé, Tasso Katselas. And, you would be amazed to learn that Bill was the entrepreneurial driving force behind the creation of the MCG's state-of-the-art concert hall and recording studio, a venue that has attracted the world's top names in jazz music, including Dizzy Gillespie, Betty Carter, Herbie Hancock, Mc-Coy Tyner, and many, many more. You would have to conclude that Bill Strickland is a man who deals in surprises—surprises of the positive sort, surprises that not only open people's eyes, but their hearts, as well.

And you would be right.

Bill states his calling with pinpoint clarity: *seeing life as a set of possibilities, not as a set of limitations.* He believes that if you provide people with a range of human experiences, intelligently presented and administered properly, they will change their lives. "Because they'll see themselves as contributors," he says, "As assets instead of liabilities."

Most of the students at Bidwell have been told at one time or another that they are liabilities. Bill's school turns them around and gives them—often for the first time in their lives—the sense that they matter, that they are worthwhile, that they have a future. You walk into the building and you can sense this. There are some 400 students hard at work in a dozen classes, but the hallways are quiet. The building hums with focused activity. You peek into the classrooms—a state-of-the-art chemical laboratory, a fully-equipped computer facility, one of the world's only culinary amphitheaters, a complete digital recording studio—and you see students paying rapt attention to instructors or working independently on projects of their own. The place is immaculate, with beautiful paintings and sculpture throughout, and an in-house art gallery showcasing the work of world-renowned artists. A bright atrium welcomes you as you enter; hallways spider out gracefully from this center space. A large dining area with impressive windows lies beyond; it resembles an executive conference center at a four-star resort. The food, prepared by gourmet chefs, completes the picture. You feel you are in a successful high-tech corporation, not a vocational school, and the sense of respect that permeates the environment translates into how students and teachers treat each other and themselves.

In overseeing Bidwell's design, Bill made these choices quite consciously. His ambition was to build a magnificent place in the inner city for people whose lives often are not that pretty. "I wanted to build a building like this, to show people that it could be done anywhere. I built the whole school around that philosophy: a beautiful place with good food, lots of light, with people who care. To show that the experience that I had was transferable to others. The ghetto is not the neighborhood," he says. "It's a state of mind."

Bill escaped that state of mind as an adolescent when he discovered ceramic arts under the guidance of his high school teacher, Frank Ross. "My life changed when I made a big old pot. The arts saved my life," he admits. "Because before that, I didn't have a focus. And, as a black kid growing up in a neighborhood like I did, you've got three career choices without a focus: jail, drugs, or death. The arts gave me a bridge to walk across to a new life. They gave me a new relationship to myself and to the community. When I invested in the arts, I invested in life."

At the Manchester Craftsmen's Guild, Bill helps young people make that same investment every day. "My constituency is here," he says. "I've got the guys walking around with the shoes untied and the pants falling down to here. I've got white working-class kids here. Hispanic teens. Unemployed adults. They're all here. The representation of the world is in this building. And I made that a point before I got this far. I decided that people biologically are built the same. We have different complexions, but on the inside, we're alike. And we all respond universally to the same things. Whether it's a poor black kid or a poor white kid or a middle-class adult, they all need affection. And they all need good food. And they all need an aesthetic in their life. And the ability to feel like they're worth something."

Sometimes young people come to Bidwell or the Craftsmen's Guild with that essential ability to feel like they're worth something driven out of them. That is when, Bill says, you have to revive it in them. "And that is what," he adds, "this place does as well or better than many I've seen around the country."

And Bill has seen a lot. He's constantly in demand from major corporations, social service agencies, and private foundations to consult with them on how they can recreate the success he has achieved. His theory, though, is really quite simple. "Things grow out of things," he says. "You put bright people together, give them enough to eat and a good building and the funding and then get out of the way—because that is where you'll get innovation. A lot of the things we do grow out of the learning and innovation that come from one set of experiences."

Bill's work and his calling are one. He knew that he had made his decision to stay where he is some years ago when he turned down the opportunity to fly commercial jets. (He is an airline pilot, too—another one of those surprises.) It was something he wanted to do very badly, but he decided not to go. He wanted to continue making his dream for Bidwell and the Guild a reality. It became obvious to him that the true expression of his calling was to be found on the ground, not in the air.

The One-Year Test

The truest gauge of someone's alignment with calling is the "one-year test." When we asked Bill what he would do if he found out he had just one year to live, he responded without hesitation. "I'd do the same thing I did before. I wouldn't change anything. I'd probably do more of it. But the thing would be the same. I'd get up and come to work here. And I'd be selling the same bill of goods I'm selling now. Which is all the stuff that I do. The clay. Photography. Music. Architecture. So nothing would change in that regard. I wouldn't say,

'Well, I've only got a year left, so I'd better stop and go on to what's really happening. This *is* what's happening."

And Bill is deeply committed to making it happen around the world. His vision for the future is to build at least a hundred centers like his in the United States and a similar number around the world—centers that are all characterized by high quality architecture, world-class facilities, world-class staff, world-class food, great music, lots of art, and lots of technology. Bill's plan is to build them right on the edge of the worst neighborhoods and start using the centers as a way to revitalize those communities and the lives of the people in them. He says he has no intention of changing that vision and is absolutely confident he has the know-how and connections to make it happen. When you realize this know-how grows out of his current success and that those connections include places like Harvard, Kellogg, IBM, Bayer, Starbucks, American Express, and more, you begin to believe. And you begin to understand the power of calling in one's work.

This powerful sense of calling resonates through Bill's life. He says he would like to be remembered as a guy who absolutely refused to see life as anything but hopeful and as a wealth of human possibilities. In spite of the difficulties life presents all of us, Bill says, "I believe that there is something very special and very precious and very transforming about engaging life in terms of dreams rather than nightmares." He sees his contribution as helping to let everyone know that they can do the kind of work he does—work that is life-affirming and positive and that gives back to the larger community. "That is my contribution to enhancing life on the planet, which I believe is what your ultimate stewardship is. The ultimate way of thanking life for being what it is, is to help pass it on to the next group."

Obviously, Bill is passing on a lot. His initial dream for Bid-well/MCG has become a reality, and has made dreams come alive for countless numbers of students as well as the community-at-large. And it all started with that initial sensation of calling, that sense Bill first had when art saved his life back in high school.

What about you? Do you have a sense of calling about your work? Do you believe you are doing what you were always meant to do? If you had a year to live, would you keep doing what you are doing? Would you give it away for free? Or are you called to something else entirely?

Perhaps most importantly, are you, like Bill Strickland, applying your gifts on something you are passionate about? Are the things that you do in your work the kinds of things that spring naturally from who you are? Do you feel them in your bones, deeply, in the marrow of your bones? We need to utilize our gifts to feel satisfaction in our work. Reimagining work, therefore, is, to a great degree, a matter of identifying our gifts and putting them to use in service of our calling.

Making Work Work

Be honest: if you won the lottery, what would you do?

Most of us—those telling the truth, anyway—admit we would quit our jobs. But then what? Lie on a beach drinking piña coladas for the rest of our days? Maybe for a while, but after some time, that, too, would start to get old.

The simple truth is, even if we did not need to work, we would still have to—in some form or another. We are hard-wired, as human beings, to be engaged. We are compelled to contribute, whether we need to or not.

The eighteenth-century German philosopher, Immanuel Kant, argued that it was irrational, and therefore, in his view, immoral, for a people to let their "talents rust"; we are obliged, he says, to seek to improve ourselves out of the very same impulse that motivates our survival instinct. You do not have to buy Kant's moral philosophy to agree on the necessity of bettering ourselves; as he implies, the daily act of feeding ourselves is evidence of our desire for self-improvement.

Point being: we work; that is what we do. Even if we did not, we would. Even when we do not, or cannot, we are.

Unfortunately, many of us are too busy at our jobs to recognize this. We're so consumed by taking care of business that we overlook the most important aspect of what we do: that it IS what we do and that we have only one life in which to do it.

It all comes down, as we have said many times in many ways, to a sense of purpose, a feeling that we are doing something that makes a difference—at least in some small way—to something we care about.

It does not have to be world-changing; it need not be lucrative, or beautiful, or even something your parents would approve of. It just has to connect you with yourself and, by extension, to people you care about, your "kin," or what we might call your "tribe."

When work does that, it works.

The nineteenth century British philosopher, John Stuart Mill said it well when he described his conception of happiness. A life well-lived, he argued, is not one of continual joy, for no such life is possible; rather, happiness, according to Mill, is best understood "as not a life of rapture, but moments of such, in an existence made up of few and transitory pains, many and various pleasures, with a decided predominance of the active over the passive, and having as the foundation of the whole, not to expect more from life than it is capable of bestowing."

The idea is that it starts with an attitude toward life that is realistic, but hopeful. We cannot expect everything from life all the time, but we can, by taking action, make the best life possible given the constraints and realities we face. Certainly, this is the case with work. Nothing we do is going to be pure joy every single moment of every single day. But if we can understand the place of work in our overall happiness and contribute accordingly, we will be met with unexpected levels of overall satisfaction in the long run.

As we mentioned earlier, the Ancient Greek philosopher Aristotle knew this well. Happiness, or *eudaimonia*, was, for Aristotle, a kind of activity, not a state of being. To be happy meant performing the characteristic human activity—our *telos*, our purpose or end—in a manner consistent with virtue. And since human beings are distinguished among all other forms of life by our ability to reason, this means that our purpose, our unique virtue, is rational activity. Happiness, then, becomes a matter of reasoning well in order to live well—doing what we are meant to do and doing it well. Some three thousand years later, here we are, in this book, saying essentially the same thing.

It has been said that all of Western philosophy is just footnotes to Plato; perhaps that should include footnotes to Aristotle, as well.

Fully Absorbed and Immersed

There is an exercise called "the egg-drop game" that you may have played in school or in a seminar. Teams are given ten drinking straws, some masking tape, and a raw egg; their challenge is to create a device—using only the straws and tape—that will enable the egg to be dropped from a height of eight feet without breaking. It is a fascinating and, invariably, quite fun activity. Participants really get into it and work hard on their designs. And, it does not matter whether the teams are composed of sixth graders or corporate executives; the same thing happens—time flies. No matter how long teams are given to work on their projects, there are always a couple of groups that wish they had more time. What is interesting to see is how differently teams behave when they are making their egg-dropper and when they are not.

Students in Vicky Hutchings' sixth grade class at Whitman Middle School in Seattle, Washington, are, like most sixth graders, notoriously squirrelly. Most of the time, they sit at their desks halfway paying attention to their teacher, whispering, writing notes, drawing pictures, and surreptitiously sneaking glances at comic books tucked inside the text they are supposed to be following. But when they are building their egg-droppers, they are all business. Each student is focused on the task at hand.

They talk, but the conversations are about better ways to attach straws or more effective techniques to soften the impact on the egg. Discipline problems disappear; in fact, students tend to get annoyed if anyone acts disruptively. You pretty much have to tear them away from their projects when it is time to do the drop test. Some groups, given the freedom to do so, would spend all day designing and redesigning their egg-drop gizmo.

What is it about this activity that makes it so different than so much of what students do the rest of the time? Well, for one thing, it is not graded—and there is no homework. But more importantly, participants in the egg-drop game care about the process and the results. They want to do well, not because their teacher or parents say they should, but because *they want to.* Something about the activity compels them to really engage with it. For one thing, it is fun, and for another, it is hilarious to potentially see a dozen eggs smashed to smithereens in the classroom, but there is more to it than that. Students commit to the exercise because it gives them an opportunity to express themselves in any number of ways. Those with an engineering bent are drawn to the challenge of designing an effective safety device, those with a flair for the artistic like the chance to make something interesting looking, those who are more people-oriented appreciate the opportunity to work as a team. There is something in it for nearly everyone, something that appeals to something that is in nearly every student: their calling—giving their gifts away to something they are passionate about in an environment that fits their values.

The call to a particular way of work fulfills four essential needs. First, it fulfills the need to feel engaged with something larger than us. What is important is that we feel we are responding to a wisdom that is greater than our own. It is the experience of doing something that just "feels right," even if we do not know why. Second, being called fulfills our ongoing need to make a difference in the world. Bill Strickland felt this need powerfully at an early age; yet his call to work with young people in disadvantaged communities continued and continues to evolve in stages over his lifetime. Third, responding to calling fulfills our need to become as much as we can be. Whether we are conscious of it or not, we all have a strong desire to maximize our potential. Nothing satisfies this desire more fully than activities performed out of a sense of calling. Doing work that is consistent with our calling involves a conscious choice to be ourselves—to reveal our gifts to us and to the world. Finally, the call to a particular life's work fulfills our need to leave a legacy. Calling is a unifying story that brings together the social, individual, and sacred dimensions of our lives. It connects us to our communities, ourselves, and as Bill Strickland's story illustrates, it connects us to all that really matters.

The question is: how can we experience a similar sense of connection to our work? And perhaps more importantly, how will we feel when we do?

Passion in Work

What inspires you? What consistently intrigues you, makes you excited to explore, gives you energy and leads you to action? What, in other words, is your reason for getting up in the morning?

The answer to these questions provides insights into our passions—the causes we care most about and are drawn inevitably to engage with. As we undertake a full reimagining of work, identifying our passions is key.

But how do we find passion in work? How do we achieve a connectedness to broader concerns? How do we commit to something larger than ourselves such that we feel an overwhelming sense of aliveness and purpose?

Arthur Rouner's story addresses these questions.

Ministry of Presence

At eighty-four years of age, Arthur Rouner cuts a handsome figure as he warmly takes your hand and pumps it, causing the forty African bracelets he wears on his wrists to jangle merrily. Arthur calls them his "prayer beads" and explains how a friend from the Pokot tribe in Kenya gave him his first one. He has since added a new bracelet on every trip to Africa. "They remind me to pray for my friends there," he says.

Arthur and his wife, Molly, are the founders of the Pilgrim Center for Reconciliation, based in Minneapolis, Minnesota. As he discusses the work of reconciliation—"most people have at least one relationship where there is a wound"—you get the feeling that you are with a man who knows who he is, why he is here, and where he is going—man who has a powerful sense of his calling.

He says that his life of Christian ministry chose him. "My father made it clear," he states, "that he wanted me to be a minister, like him." But Arthur's real calling did not come to him in church. It came to him as a seventeen-year-old, on a merchant boat returning from Greece. The oiler on the ship was in desperate shape after returning from a weekend of carousing on shore leave. Suffering from chronic syphilis, exacerbated by dehydration, the oiler pleaded with Arthur and a small group of young men on the boat: "What is going to happen to me? What does it all mean?"

The oiler's pleas touched Arthur deeply. He did not have answers to the sailor's question, but they resonated powerfully with his own inquiries. That night, alone on the bow of the ship, Arthur heard his calling as clearly as he did the waves below: his own life's work was to serve the poor, to build bridges to people like the oiler. He vividly recalls that night and where it seemed the call came from. "I didn't hear a voice speaking to me across the ocean. It was an inner voice."

Arthur was called to Colonial Church in Edina, Minnesota, to do reconciliation work—to "build bridges." For thirty-two years, he was absorbed in a pioneering ministry, building bridges between rich and poor, inner-city and suburb, well-fed and hungry, Africa and America. Arthur's legacy at Colonial was, in his own words, "He loved the people." The feeling of absorbedness was overwhelming. "It was an awesome thing to feel that I was in the grip of God as His messenger," says Arthur.

Since leaving Colonial Church, Arthur has continued to build bridges around the world—usually in places where the chasms between people would seem to most of us insurmountable. There is no more vivid illustration of this than Arthur's work in the African nations of Kenya, Uganda, Burundi, the Central African Republic, and, perhaps most poignantly, Rwanda. He shared the world's horror at the genocidal massacre of nearly a million people there during the mid 1990s. *Time Magazine* reported that a depth of evil so searing to the soul as to be incomprehensible to our consciousness had overtaken that land. Rwanda's need—overlooked by many of the world's governments until it was too late—called to Arthur. He believed that, in the aftermath of the killings, what people were desperate for was forgiveness. For reconciliation to take place, both Hutu and Tutsi factions, perpetrators and victims alike, needed a way to forgive each other, and themselves. Unless the entire population could find a way to do this, the people in this small nation, with such a horrendous history of pain and suffering, could simply not live together.

Arthur felt that if the Church in Rwanda was to play a healing role, the church leaders themselves would need to have their own hearts healed. Their own grief and guilt and fear would have to be lifted if they were to lift those feelings from others. And in fact, as Arthur came in contact with more of these leaders, he heard a common refrain: "But how can we do the good work of reconciliation that we have been told to do if we are not healed ourselves?"

"It was precisely this healing of the inner heart that God has given to the Pilgrim Center," says Arthur. "And this call we have heard in our hearts."

It is a call to go to the killing fields in Rwanda and Burundi and to sit with the people, loving them and listening to their pain. It is a call to offer them whatever comfort is possible in the long process of healing a whole country. The Pilgrim Center invites healers in Rwanda—pastors, women's group organizers, youth leaders—"come away from the struggle and rest awhile." As Arthur observes of these people, "They are so haunted. There is no rest for them."

A youth leader in Burundi confessed early in a Pilgrim retreat, "My brother was killed in the genocide. I know who killed him. I see him around the town. I hate him. I am tempted to revenge." But at the end of retreat with the Pilgrim Center, he said, "I can hardly wait to get back home. I am going to seek out my brother's killer and tell him, 'I have forgiven you.'"

Arthur calls his life's work "a ministry of presence." His passion today is to be a genuine presence to those in need—to listen, to feel, to be reasonable and helpful to people. He sums up his ministry of presence by paraphrasing Edwin Markham:

"I just want to be a house by the side of the road where I can be a friend to man."

Arthur's passion—the essence of his calling—is to build bridges. When he discovered he could no longer do this work in the Church, he realized he had to leave his parish. He had no choice but to honor this more basic and powerful spirit emanating from within. He says that this intimate contact with the source of his calling is his awareness of God. It has always been—and remains—more important than any institution or formal structure. Arthur's life work, and the mission of the Pilgrim Center, has no agenda, he says, other than the Holy Spirit's agenda. He describes it simply. "There are no fancy notebooks, no experts, no raised platforms for 'important people.' Instead, we all sit together in a circle, gathered literally around the cross."

Igniting Passion

"Passion" is a loaded word in our culture. It connotes sexuality, emotion, lack of inhibition, uncontrolled self-expression, wildness; in short, it suggests danger. We are told from an early age to control our passions, to suppress them. Passion is like fire, goes the story. It burns brightly at first and then dies out, and unless we are cautious, passion will harm us. The fire is not to be toyed with; better to steer clear of passion altogether if we can.

None of these characterizations of passion capture the reality of passion as it relates to calling. When we refer to passion, we *are* referring to a kind of freedom, but it is a freedom that is life-affirming and positive. Rather than representing an expression of just a single part of our character, like sexuality, passion relates to the full expression of who we are. Moreover, passion is not something that ignites once, flares up quickly, and then dies away. Passion may not catch fire for some time; it may not take hold until there is a complete awareness of what we are passionate about. And, properly nourished, passion can burn throughout the entire course of our lives.

CHAPTER 5

Reimagining Values— Where Do You Do It?

"It's Only a Job"

My taxi driver looks exhausted. I have to tap on the window three times to get his attention before he opens the door for me. Coming around to take my bags, he shakes his head and squints, clearing cobwebs from his brain. When he slides back into the driver's seat, I can see in the rearview mirror how red and watery his eyes are.

"Where to?" he mumbles in a heavy accent made heavier by a thick sleepy tongue.

"Home," I say, leaning back into the seat, but—somewhat concerned about my driver—not quite relaxing. For one thing, it makes me nervous to see his eyelids droop as I give him directions to my house.

"Ah, home," says the driver, wistfully as he merges into traffic. "Very nice. I haven't been to my home in five years."

Figuring that he'll be more likely to stay awake if he's talking, I take the opportunity to engage him in conversation.

"Really? Where's home?"

"Far away," he tells me, "Far, far away."

A few moments pass. I can't tell if my driver is remembering his country or nodding off. I try to keep the conversational ball rolling.

"So what brings you here?"

"Many problems in my home country," he says. "I come here to get away. For a better life."

"And how has it worked out?"

A smile creeps across his face. "In my home country, I am a teacher. At University. Here, I am a taxi driver. I drive sixteen hours a day, sometimes every day of the week."

"Not so well, then," I surmise.

"No," He laughs. "It is not so bad."

An eighteen-wheel semi truck looms large in the windshield. I hold my breath as my driver swings wide around him. When my heart returns to my chest, I ask another question.

"You ever think about going back?"

"Oh, I miss it," he replies. "But no. Too many problems there. Too much restriction. Here, at least, I can say what I think. And my family doesn't fear the knock on the door in the middle of the night."

"But what about your career? Your work? Don't you mind driving a taxi?"

The driver cuts across four lanes of traffic to my exit. He shrugs his shoulders and looks at me in the mirror. "It is only a job. Not so important. I cannot work as a teacher in this country and so this is how I make money for my family. That is all. What matters is that we are safe and free. When my son grows up maybe he will be a teacher himself. At least he has that chance. So I work this job. It is my choice."

"You don't feel cheated somehow? Like you're not getting what you want out of life?"

"On the contrary, my friend. Life is not so much about getting as it is about giving. And the choice I make now allows me to give what I must give. Other things are more important to me than being a teacher—being a father, a husband, a friend. With this job, I can do those, and so, it is good."

As I give the driver a few final directions and he pulls up at my house, I look at him more closely. There is a quiet calm about him I hadn't noticed before. His eyes contain a spark that even exhaustion cannot extinguish.

He helps me with my bags; I pay him. He ducks back into the cab and heads off. I think I would have liked to correct him about one thing: even in this country, he is still a teacher.

Try to imagine if you were in this cabdriver's shoes.

Would you be so accepting of your situation? Would you have the same sense of perspective about life? Would you be as clear about why you are doing what you are doing and as positive about prospects for the future?

Would you, in other words, be as clear about your values as he was?

Many of us probably would not be. We are not nearly so settled in our understanding of why we are doing what we are doing. We make choices and compromises without feeling satisfied that these choices and compromises are worth it. This implies that we are disconnected from our values—and that it is valuable to reconnect to them in a deeper way.

Who's Dealing the Cards?

Think of how often we complain about the hand life has dealt us. But when we do, we forget who's dealing the cards—it's us!

Remember the game "Hand Dealt." The sixth-graders who played it considered the hands they had been dealt unfair primarily because they were not the ones dealing.

When we play the game with kids, though, we always follow up the initial round with two others. Players—especially those who were dealt undesirable lives—always insist we redeal the cards. So, we do. We collect all the job, relationship, and living situation cards and, after shuffling them up, deal them out once more. Inevitably, the same dissatisfactions ensue as in the first round, just with different people. Players who have gotten bad jobs once again complain that life has dealt them a lousy hand; they chafe at having to settle for a life that is not of their own making.

So, in the third round, we give them the opportunity to design their own cards. Instead of dealing the cards out, students create jobs, relationships, and living situations for themselves. Of course, this means we end up with an inordinate number of professional athletes and CEOs in the room, but that is just the point. When young people are not forced to settle for situations that are imposed upon them, they tend to dream big. They tend to envision their lives as grand adventures to be lived to their fullest. They tend not to settle for the something small; rather, they imagine that they can be whatever they want to be, however unlikely it may seem as a real possibility. And their choices unabashedly reflect the thing they most love doing, whether it is art, sports, community service, you name it. Unconstrained by externally imposed limitations, the kids come up with their dream lives and at the core of these dreams is the internal fire we refer to as calling.

When they have the chance to deal their "lives" out to themselves—when they are allowed to choose the cards they are dealt—they feel that their "lives" were fair. But when their ability to make choices is constrained, they feel trapped. They feel like even a desirable life is not really desirable.

Most of us are not nearly so trapped in the game we are playing as we think. We *can* make choices and changes that more accurately reflect our deepest values. We do not have to live in a manner that is inconsistent with what we really care about. We have the freedom to structure our lives so that the burdens we accept are burdens we find acceptable. Like the taxi driver, we can learn to make choices that represent values we truly consider valuable.

The first step in doing that is to be absolutely sure what our values really are.

Do I Value My Values?

Values, as we mentioned earlier, are active. Valuing is something we *do*. The reason one of our values *is* a value is that we *live* it.

We express our values through the choices we make. Consequently, if we are living in a manner that is consistent with our values, our values will be apparent in the way that we live. The *environment* in which we work, for example, will reflect the kinds of things we care about. The way we spend our time and money and the friendships we cultivate are other ways we make our values apparent in the world.

At least, that is the theory.

In fact, many of us at one time or another have made choices that are decidedly at odds with our values. Many of us have found ourselves in situations that prevent us from being who we really are. The pressure to do well—that is, make money—gets in the way of our desire to do good—that is, express our core values. When that happens, we tend to lose sight of the very values that could enable us to find ourselves. We end up in a self-reinforcing system that drags us farther away from our values, farther away from ourselves.

Dave experienced this very dynamic:

"In my early thirties, I tried my hand at a number of different jobs. At one point, I found myself doing computer network maintenance for a high-tech software development company. I'm not entirely sure how I ended up in this position; I guess I sort of fell into it through my interest at the time in computers. I had never intended to be a computer geek and even when I took the job, I hoped it would be a stepping-stone to something else. But the money was great and I enjoyed helping people use the emerging technology to do their jobs more effectively.

"It didn't take long, though, for the gap between my values—what I really cared about—and my job—what I was doing—to widen.

"For one thing, the organization put an overriding emphasis on speed. Everything had to be done yesterday, so people were always rushing around, doing six things at once, and getting incredibly stressed out. This put a lot of pressure on my job because the inevitable network hiccups inevitably caused delays and, inevitably, people blamed me for missed deadlines—even if the delay caused by the network failure was only a minor part of the slowdown.

"So I was working seven days a week constantly trying to upgrade our system, and half the time I did upgrades, something else would go wrong, and we'd be no better—if not worse—off than before. People would complain and point fingers at me and in general, make me feel pretty awful about myself. I was pretty unhappy, but oddly, I didn't even realize it. I just kept pushing harder and harder, trying to make myself fit into an environment whose values were quite different than my own. Whereas a sense of community and cooperation were of paramount concern to me, this organization valued individuality and competition above all else. I was constantly out of synch but I took it to be a failure on my part that things weren't working out. I remember one Sunday evening about eight o'clock coming into an office where a program designer was working. He seemed to be having a grand time tweaking the color palette on an image he was processing. Obsessing over the subtlest of details in a part of the program very few people were ever likely to see was, to him, a perfectly satisfying way to spend a Sunday night. I thought there must be something wrong with me that I was wishing I were at home reading a book.

"It was really just luck that I got out of this situation. My wife, Jennifer, was accepted to a graduate program in fine arts at a college in another city and we chose to move. I remember feeling awful about having to give my notice but I also recall that, as a soon as I did, I felt great. It was as if a huge burden was lifted from my shoulders. And, as a matter of fact, it was, for no sooner did I leave the job than I was able to stop carrying around a version of me that wasn't me. I was able to stop trying to force myself into a value system at odds with my own. I was able to be myself instead of someone I thought I ought to be, someone whose values were inconsistent with the things I held most dear."

Of course Dave's situation is not unique. Many of us, for one reason or another, find ourselves in working or living situations that are a poor fit for our values. The stories of how we end up like this are legion: money, family, timing may all have something to do with it. Ultimately, though, these stories are secondary. It is not so important how we got into the situation. What really matters is how can find value in it.

Acting on Values

Think of times in your own life when you have acted upon your values. Recall how it felt to stand up for what you believe in, even if it meant short-term hardship. Remember the sense of satisfaction that came from feeling connected to an idea or cause larger than yourself. There may have been financial implications; you may have had to sacrifice monetary success for successful expression of your values, but it was probably worth it. These are the experiences that make life worth living, the experiences that give meaning and purpose to our days.

To have such experiences more consistently, we have to do two things. We have to develop a deeper understanding of what our values really are and we have to begin to act in ways that express those values in our daily lives.

Keeping in mind that what makes a value into a value is that we live it, we might begin by considering some commonly-held values. Some people cleave to what are usually thought of as traditional values like security, spirituality, order, community, health, wealth, work, family, and health. Others tend to hold values such as autonomy, newness, change, freedom, excitement, teamwork, and peace. And still others may share any of these as well as values such as cooperation, relaxation, friendship, power, learning, nature, and recreation.

Think of such values. Ask yourself which you value most highly. Which of those mentioned—or which others—would you list as your true values?

Then examine your answers more carefully to see if you have identified values you *really do* value.

Check Your Checkbook

One simple way to ascertain what our values really are is to look at how we spend our money and our time. Review your checkbook (or online bank account) and your calendar for the last three months. Where has your time and money gone? What are the five things you have spent most of your time on? What are the five things you have spent most of your money on? What does this say about your values? If, for example, community, cooperation, and friendship are your core values, would it not be likely that your check stubs would include a number of entries for donations to social service organizations and dinners with friends? And your calendar would probably have dates for volunteer work groups and neighborhood parties.

If, on the other hand, you discover that the most common check you have written is to your travel agent and the most prevalent item in your datebook is an out-of-town meeting, then perhaps you *really* value something else—perhaps excitement, newness, or advancement at work.

Robert Fulghum, the best-selling author of *Everything I Need to Know I Learned in Kindergarten* and other contemporary classics was once asked how the phenomenal success of his books had changed his life. The interviewer was obviously hoping for some juicy tidbit about how Fulghum, the former minister and longtime advocate of simplicity in word and deed, had developed expensive tastes or come to expect a level of luxury that his newfound wealth had made possible.

Fulghum surprised the interviewer by responding that success basically gave him the opportunity to put his money where his mouth was. He was able to help out individuals and organizations he cared about in ways that he had not been able to previously. Instead of just providing moral support, he could provide financial support, too. In short, he was able to contribute to the success of what he valued. Money did not change his values; it only gave him new ways to express them.

The question to ask yourself, then, is if the values you act upon—your demonstrated values—are indeed those you want to act upon. It may be that they are and that the disconnect is simply between what you think you value and what you say you value. If that is the case, then all you need to do is change your way of speaking.

Many of us may have experienced something like this when we have gone through a major job transition. We continue to tell ourselves, and others, that we are one way when our actions indicate that we are another. In the case of seeking a new job, for instance, we may loudly bemoan our working social life simultaneously hunting for exactly the same sort of situation in which we find ourselves.

If your demonstrated values are at odds with the values you would choose to work by, then it is necessary to make some new choices. It is necessary to, at least, begin spending your time, your money, and your energy at work in different ways. This means you actually have to do things differently—not just think about doing them differently. And that can be difficult.

Suppose, for instance, that, after reviewing your checkbook and calendar, you find that spending far more time and money on shopping for new clothes, furniture, and computer gear than you would have expected—given that your stated values are simplicity and thrift. And suppose you believe that these demonstrated values—which seem to be more about status and wealth—are not what you want your life to be about; they are not the gift you want to give to the world. In this case, you will have to find new interests, new ways of being, and a new way of work. You will not be able to go to the mall as often; you will not be able to spend your time shopping online. It may be a painful transition; you may have to get some help or counseling to shift your life's direction. But if that is what you want your life to be about, then presumably, it is worth it.

Of course, no one is forcing you to change except you. If you do not want to, you do not have to. But if you do...then what other choice do you have?

Well, It's Easy for You...

People who are dissatisfied with their jobs often say to people who love their work, "Oh, well, it's easy for *you*. You have the perfect job. You're a writer. Or an artist. Or you have your own company. No wonder you're happy. Me, I'm just a pitiful wage slave for a multinational cartel. If I were in your shoes, I wouldn't complain, either."

What these people do not realize, though, is that there are no perfect jobs. No matter what you do—even if you are a rock star or a supermodel—there will be aspects of your work that are less than thrilling. What makes a job great is not so much *what* you do, but *how* you do it. It is a matter of "fit"—the alignment between your inner self and outer activities. In short, it is a matter of connecting who you are with what you do.

We know this intuitively. We are all aware that the same task, performed one day, can feel very different the next. Answering customer service calls on Monday morning gives us the sense that we are making a difference in the world; by Friday afternoon, it is all we can do to keep from diving into the receiver and strangling the person on the other end. So what has changed? Not the job—it is the same as ever. Not the customers—their questions and concerns are just as they were. No, it is something about *us* that is different, something about our attitude toward what we're doing that changes everything.

It is true that creative, self-directed people—artists, writers, entrepreneurs—are more likely to feel this way about their work than the average wage-earner, but that is not primarily because they are artists, writers, or entrepreneurs. (Think of examples like Van Gogh or Hemingway or Sylvia Plath, who, despite their artistic successes, were deeply conflicted in their lives.) Rather, it is primarily because they chose their life's work—they heeded their calling. Having a sense of creative control over one's work and life makes us more likely to feel that our efforts are meaningful and worthwhile.

The challenge, then, is to develop that sense of choice within the context of one's job—even if we are not writers, artists, or entrepreneurs—even if we are "just" customer service representatives answering consumer questions Monday morning through Friday afternoon.

Connectedness and Contribution

One way to begin doing that is to reflect upon those moments within our working lives during which we have felt particularly energized. Nearly everyone experiences—at least occasionally—that on-the-job sensation of connectedness and contribution to something truly meaningful. In these moments—however fleeting—we can begin to find the essence of our essential calling. And we can use them to explore ways to expand the scope of these moments outward so they begin to occupy as much of our time at work as possible.

Of course, changing one's mindset is not as easy as changing one's clothes. Most of us cannot suddenly decide to love something we were only recently ambivalent about. On the other hand, it is certainly not impossible to modify our outlook on things. We are all familiar with instances where we were able to change a barely tolerable situation into something fairly enjoyable just by adjusting our attitude. Dave says, "I worked at a company that had a one hour staff meeting every Friday afternoon at 3:00. I hated them because they seemed like such a waste of time; I thought of them as unnecessary and boring bitch sessions. My boss, though, sensing my discomfort with them, suggested that I view the meetings as opportunities for increasing my understanding of the challenges people were

facing and for learning more about the way individuals responded to business challenges in real time. He also assigned
me the task of writing a one-page summary of the meeting
to be distributed company-wide. I so enjoyed that task that it
eventually developed into an organizational newsletter that
I became editor of. What had once been an onerous burden
eventually transformed into one of the central—and most enjoyable—aspects of my entire job."

It would seem from this example, there are at least two
parts to changing our mindset about the less desirable aspects
of our jobs. First, and probably most importantly, we have to
want to change. Desire is key, and can make all the difference.
In Dave's example, he was asked by his boss to modify his perspective. The possibility of letting his company down provided
some impetus for looking at things differently. He wanted to
make a good impression on the person who signed his checks;
it is not surprising that it was not particularly difficult for him
to find the desire to change his attitude about the meetings.
The incentive was right there in the form of his paycheck. It is
not so difficult to learn to like something when doing so is so
obviously in our self-interest.

What is useful to recognize, therefore, is that—in the
broadest sense—it is *always* in our self-interest to learn to better like the less likable aspects of our jobs. This does not, of
course, include any aspects that are illegal or abusive, but it
does pertain to the vast majority of slightly annoying or un-
comfortable parts of our workdays. Our lives, after all, are all
that we have. If we are spending our precious hours feeling
half-alive as we drag ourselves through tasks that we abhor,
then we are wasting our most precious commodity of all: time.

If, by contrast, we can shift our perspective on things so that those hours are expended on something that—at least—is in keeping with our deepest convictions and desires, then we will feel more alive and more integrated into our daily activities. So, the incentive exists to make a positive change in our attitudes about all parts of our jobs—even without our bosses telling us to.

The second part about changing our attitudes towards the less desirable aspect of our jobs—or our lives, for that matter— is that we need to develop some sort of plan for doing things differently. If we do not change our behavior, then nothing will change. As the late Larry Wilson, corporate training guru and master salesperson, puts it, "If you always do what you've always done, you'll always get what you've always gotten." And if what we've always gotten is dissatisfaction, then, by all means, we will continue being dissatisfied if we still behave in the ways that have led us to dissatisfaction—no matter how differently we think about them.

The Dalai Lama, in his book, *Ethics for the New Millennium,* says that we can classify the actions we take in pursuit of happiness into those which make a positive contribution to that pursuit and those which make a negative contribution to it. He then points out that those activities which foster happiness have, as their ultimate basis, concern for both the short-term benefit to us and the long-term effects on others' happiness. In short, he argues, genuine peace of mind is only possible when we undertake actions that are inspired by the wish to help others. We also find, he writes, that when we act out of concern for others, the peace this creates in our own hearts brings peace to our families, friends, workplaces, communities, and the world. Our ability, as humans to feel compassion and love, says the Dalai Lama, is a precious gift, perhaps the most precious of all.

Surprisingly, this is fairly easy to see within the context of our working lives. When we feel like we are helping others—be they customers, coworkers, or prospective clients—our level of work fulfillment increases significantly. By contrast, when we are doing something that seems like it benefits only ourselves, we tend to feel less than completely fulfilled. It continually comes back to a question of values: if we are fulfilling the urge to give our gifts away to others in an environment that is consistent with what we really do value, then we feel most fulfilled. When we live our lives in conscious connection to calling, we truly come alive.

CHAPTER 6

....

Reimagining Legacy—
Have You Played Your Music?

Did I Play My Music?

"Did I live a good life?" "Did my life matter?" "Did I play my music?"

The answers to questions like these reveal our legacy—our "leave behind,"—our footprint, the music that plays after we are gone. When we explore our legacy we ask "what do we want our lives to have been about?"

When older adults look back upon their lives, they consistently express a hope that their existence has made a difference. Most do not fear dying nearly as much they do the prospect of having lived a meaningless life. We want to have made some "small dent" in the world. The prospect that no one will remember us after we are gone or worse, that no one will even notice, is deeply unsettling.

Our legacy emerges from a life that is lived in a manner consistent with our calling. When we have given our gifts away in service to something we are passionate about in an environment that supports our values, we leave a legacy that is meaningful and makes a positive difference to our loved ones and us.

To explore more fully your thinking about legacy, ask yourself: *Is there something larger than my own life that I care about?*

Oliver Wendell Holmes said "most people go to their graves with their music still inside them." This is a crying shame; every one of us has a song to sing, a melody to contribute to the world's symphony. That anyone should miss the opportunity to contribute his or her unique voice is heartbreaking; that so many fail to make their offer is nothing short of tragic.

Why then, do so many people die with their songs unsung? The reasons are legion. Lack of time, lack of clarity, lack of confidence all contribute to the collective silence. Unexpected responsibilities, illnesses, or changes in family situations cause many people to postpone living. But the most common reason that people go to their graves with their music still inside them is that they never really come to know what their music is. They never really identify their song. They remain unclear, in other words, about their calling. They may, in fact, be whistling—loud and hard—but the tune they are following is not their authentic melody at all.

In the 1995 movie *Mr. Holland's Opus* Richard Dreyfus plays Glen Holland, a high school music teacher who begins his career thinking of it as nothing more than a way to make money while he works on his "real work" of composing. As the film follows him through some thirty years of teaching, we come to realize—and more importantly, Mr. Holland comes to realize—that his true opus is the contribution he makes to his students' lives. His song is not so much to be a composer of music as to be a composer of dreams. Although it takes him many years to understand this, the revelation, when it does come, is a source of deep satisfaction and pride.

To discover our own music requires some of the discipline that learning to play any song proficiently does. We have to acquaint ourselves with our own internal score and practice diligently. We have to explore new themes and modes of expression on a regular basis. And we have to be willing to make the sometimes less than perfectly harmonious sounds that are produced by the instruments of beginning musicians.

What Is My Music?

What is your "music" to play? Are you playing it or is still inside? How can you let it out more consistently? How can you whistle your own tune?

Understanding of our calling—the blending together of our gifts, passions, and values—is heightened by focusing on those three qualities in greater depth. Our Calling Card helps us envision where our lives are headed; exploring our gifts, passions, and values helps us guide us forward in a manner that will be as natural and fulfilling as possible.

Earlier, we referred to the famous Oliver Wendell Holmes quote: "Many people die with their music still in them. Why is this so? Too often it happens because they are always getting ready to live. Before they know it, time runs out."

Our music is our legacy, what we leave behind to the world, the tune that carries on after we are gone. If we die with that music still within us, our legacy is silenced in some ways. As we reimagine work and our relationship to it, we benefit from considering how we can let our music be heard while we live, so it can continue to play even when we are no more.

It is an issue that gets to the heart of calling. What do you want to leave behind as the legacy of your years of work? What would you like people to say about you and what you did? When we heed our life's calling, we make something more of our life than just our life. We spill over the edges of our allotted time and make a difference for the ages. In short, we leave a legacy that carries on after we are gone.

Actually, to be honest, we leave a legacy no matter what we do. The choices we made define the person we were whether we like it or not. It is just that some people leave legacies that express their *true* selves, while others simply leave an unfinished tune that signifies little of what they were really about.

What Is My "Inner Urge"?

Many voices call to us during our lives; most will not resonate with the sound of our calling. We are challenged, therefore, to decide which call to heed, and when.

The idea of calling includes a commitment to be moved by something other than simple self-interest. Calling by its definition—the inner urge to give our gifts away—is a dedication to something larger than us. Calling means replacing selfishness with selflessness.

How does your work help others? How is your work an expression of service?

No matter what people do for a living—no matter how we pay the bills—we all want to feel good about our work. We want it to count for something. We want it to express who we are. We do not want to waste our precious time on earth doing something meaningless. We want to feel that, at least in some small way, our work contributes to making the world a better place. This urge is fulfilled only when what we do makes a positive difference in someone else's life.

As we search to uncover that "inner urge to give our gifts away"—our calling—we are apt to make many false starts and wrong turns. All of us will experience embarrassing failures at some point. Most of us will change jobs and careers many times as we seek expression of our vocational voice. All of these steps and missteps, seen from the point of view of our legacy, represent an unfolding of our calling in the world.

When we uncover our inner urge, we find ourselves becoming aware of the legacy we are leaving through our work. We develop a deeper appreciation for the ways we can serve others. We feel free to bring our values to work, to take a stand for what we believe, to be the same person on the job as we are away from it. We simply refuse to check ourselves at the workplace door. As we grow whole through heeding our calling, we bring our whole selves to our work.

Living Our Legacy Today

Think of people who have brought their whole selves to their life's work, people like Arthur Rouner or Bill Strickland. Think of how their legacies extend far beyond the scope of their lives. The effect that they have had—and continue to have—on people's lives cannot be measured in terms of a single lifetime. Their contributions to humanity ripple out and touch people in ways that no one person could possibly imagine doing. But because they are living a *legacy*, their abilities to make a difference are virtually unlimited. The music they are playing during their lives will continue on after they are gone, touching people's lives in truly unexpected ways.

Of course, you do not have to "change the world" to leave a legacy. Individuals from all walks of life lead lives whose positive influence resonates after they are gone. Many of us recall parents or grandparents, none of them famous, whose model we aspire to and whose legacies guide us. What most of these people have in common is that they brought their whole selves to what they were doing. The source of this is a powerful spirit in their lives—articulated or not—which demonstrates that all life is connected.

What is also important to realize about legacy is that it does not need to be inspired by a grand cause. Our legacy is *our* legacy; what we are called to do is unique to who we are. The following story from Richard is a perfect illustration:

I've just finished a delicious African feast at a favorite hole-in-the-wall hideaway in Nairobi, Kenya. My taxi driver, a laughing grandmother, is driving me slowly back to my hotel. Sitting in the cab, my belly full, watching the lights of the city pass by, I listen to her deep, mellifluous voice rising above the sound of the old car's engine.

She's telling me about her three grandchildren. They've been living with her since her daughter's husband was killed in an accident. That tragedy is mentioned almost as if in passing; her story focuses instead on the liveliness and energy of the three kids and what a pleasure—and a challenge—it is for her to keep up with them.

I express my condolences at her son-in-law's death and she nods sagely. Life is full of the unexpected she says. Everyday, she sees it, right here in her cab. To her, the opportunity to meet new people all the time is a source of great wonder; making connections with people, she says, is her calling. "What else matters in this world," she asks, "than people? I never tire of laughing with the happy ones and consoling the sad ones."

She tells me of the changes she's seen in Nairobi during her life. It has become a strange and dangerous city, much different from when she was a little girl. But it still has its charms for her; it is her home and she can't imagine living anywhere else.

"I am grateful anyway to be here and to have enough to eat and a job that I enjoy with its endless parade of people—young, old, rich, poor, all alone, newly-married." She tells me that her own marriage didn't work out, but she is not bitter or angry about that.

"Such is life," she shrugs. "We must look forward, not back"

Her focus is on the present; she lives very much for each day. She tells me that she drives long hours and always feels the pinch of many mouths to feed, but even when she is recounting these troubles, she radiates a joy that fills the cab. It's a joy that fills my soul as well.

It is doubtful that this taxi-driving grandmother will ever come across *Work Reimagined*, but her spirit is never far from these pages. The echo of her laughter is a ongoing reminder that when we believe our work matters, we too can radiate joy in our lives.

"Such Is Life"

In the end, what really matters, anyway? We are born, we live, we die; a thousand years from now, it is highly unlikely that any of us will be remembered. A million years from now, it is probable that the entire human race will be forgotten.

In spite of this, though, most of us feel like our lives matter. We generally think it makes a difference whether we do one thing or another. The choices that present themselves to us seem like real choices. Even though they might not affect our distant ancestors many centuries in the future, they do affect us and those around us. Our happiness, our satisfactions, our concerns—small as they are in the "such is life" scheme of things—fill up the universe from our perspective. The attention we pay to sports or fashion or even politics is evidence of how deeply we care about things that are ephemeral, if not downright insignificant.

Given, then, our ability to make mountains out of molehills combined with our perfectly reasonable concern for just making a living, it seems it might be difficult to determine what really matters and what does not—even within the context of our own lives. How can we tell whether a choice is really important or if we are just making a big deal out of something that is going to seem pointless in just a few years?

The answer is: we cannot! At least, we cannot tell for certain. All we have to do is reflect back upon how bent out of shape we got over an event in junior high school to remind us that what we take to be very important one day will seem laughably petty.

On the other hand, we can make some fairly good predictions about what sorts of things will have staying power. We can be pretty confident that some things we care about now will still seem important to us years from now. We may not be able to say with certainty that *everything* currently at the top of our lists will remain there, but—if we think about it—we are apt to do a better job of devoting ourselves to those things that really matter to us in the long run.

Life Is Beautiful

The Academy Award-winning film *Life Is Beautiful* is a poignant illustration of a calling, which in spite of being "small" in terms of its audience, is huge in terms of its meaningfulness, not only to those directly involved but also as an inspiration to others. The story centers on a loving father and his relationship with his young son. In the early years of the boy's life, the two are inseparable; they laugh, joke, play games, and delight in their mutual love for the boy's mother, for whom the father's love burns as brightly as when they first met.

Suddenly, one day, the father and son are dragged from their home and forced onto a train bound for the Nazi concentration camp Auschwitz. The remainder of the film chronicles the intense passion the father has—not only to keep his son alive, but also to keep the boy's spirit joyful through their dark ordeal. The father manages to convince his son that everyone at the camp is playing a complex game in hopes of winning a real full-sized tank as a prize. His inventiveness, humor, and dedication to his son's happiness are awe-inspiring and leave the audience deeply moved to both laughter and tears.

Although the father ultimately dies, *Life Is Beautiful* is a passionate reminder that meaning in life comes from a commitment to something larger than us. When we are absorbed in something larger than our own lives is when we feel most alive ourselves.

Victor Frankl's "logotherapy," a theory that seeks to explain and treat human behavior on the basis of meaning in life, originated from Frankl's own survival of Auschwitz. He personally observed that the people who survived prolonged imprisonment in Hitler's death camps did so because they had something beyond themselves to live for. Those who somehow managed to live through the horrors of Auschwitz cared about something else than their own lives—they had a passion for a person or a cause that sustained them. In a sense, they became absorbed in something and committed to a life larger than their own. Their survival vividly illustrates the notion that mattering matters. When we are passionately committed to a life other than our own, we are sustained in ways that are as powerful as they are unexpected.

What Makes Life Beautiful?

So, what sorts of things seem to be lastingly important?

When people look back upon their lives, nearly everyone agrees that relationships are paramount. The choices we make that sustain and nurture our caring connections with others are typically those that are least regretted. Few people look back upon their lives and wish they had spent less time with their loved ones. When all is said and done, what we cherish most, what gives our life meaning—what really matters—is the experiences we have shared with family members, friends, colleagues, clients, customers, and other members of our community.

Think about your life and work. Do not the highest highs—and the lowest lows—include others? Certainly there is much satisfaction to be taken from our own accomplishments, but those that we will take to our graves with us more often than not involve the participation of at least one other person. Our first kiss, our first heartbreak, the time our team won (or lost) the league championship, when our work group pulled an all-nighter to prepare for a major presentation, helping our children with their schoolwork, a last vacation with an aged parent—these are the events that stick with us.

Even making money lags behind. A recent study revealed what Americans think is most important in life. Just 27 percent of those surveyed said earning a lot of money was "absolutely necessary" for them to consider their lives a success, placing it far behind having strong family relationships (94 percent), having good friends (87 percent), helping people in need (87 percent), and becoming well-educated (82 percent). Clearly, those intangibles make a bigger difference to our satisfaction than how much money we make.

What this suggests is that—given a choice between doing almost anything and furthering a relationship with someone we care about—we ought to do the latter. We ought to take risks when it comes to letting people know how we feel about them. We should, in general, make that visit or place that phone call we have been meaning to.

Again, reflect upon your own experience. Which do you tend to regret more? The times you put yourself out on a limb with someone else or the times that you failed to? When you lie in bed at night, turning over all the "mistakes" you have made in life, do you agonize more about what you did not say than what you did? Is it not usually true that the only regrets we really have are the risks we *did not* take?

Wisdom of the Ages: The #1 Regret

Regularly, Richard conducts in-depth interviews with older adults—men and women in their sixties, seventies, and eighties—in which he asks them to reflect back upon their lives. He explores their memories of work and life as well as their attitudes about the choices they made or did not make in their lives. Many regret that they had not taken enough risks in their relationships; they express remorse that they were not as fearless in love as they could have been. Looking back over their lives, many express a common fear: that their lives would not, in the end, count as truly meaningful.

Their number one regret is in the area of work. They regret that they did not spend the biggest portion of their life working on things that aligned with their gifts. They fear that they have not left their own "small dent" upon the world. They are, by and large, relatively resolved about their deaths; only a few, however, are as equally comfortable about their work. Given a second chance, they would have done more to ensure that they left their distinctive marks on the world, marks that others would remember them after they were gone. What emerges as a common theme is legacy; they want to leave behind something unique, something to demonstrate that they used their gifts on something they cared about.

Many of us will admit that we share the feelings of these older adults. Their concerns are remarkably consistent with our own. Death is indeed a frightening prospect, but not nearly as frightening as the prospects associated with living—in particular, the prospect of not having lived our own authentic lives. Like the poet Dylan Thomas, we do not want to go gently into that good night; we want to rage against the dying of the light by having created a light of our own that can illuminate the way for others.

The question, of course, is how exactly do we do that? How do we truly shine so that others can light their own way forward by following our path?

Think about light for a moment and how it is generated. Anytime there is illumination, something somewhere must burn. Whether it is sunlight, candlelight, even electric light, the source is the same: excited electrons, radiation, heat. So, in order for any of us to generate our own light source, we too must burn—metaphorically, that is. We must feel a passion for something burning within us. We create light in our own lives—light that illuminates the way for others—by feeding this passion so that it burns ever more brightly.

Among the older adults that Richard has interviewed, those who had fewer regrets were those who followed their calling. Living in accordance with calling goes well beyond any financial rewards. They saw their work as an opportunity to serve others. They believed that what they did made the world a better place. It did not just satisfy their pocketbook or ego; it satisfied their soul.

Living a Legacy Life

Arthur Schindler was a German industrialist during World War II. Thanks to his efforts, many hundreds of German and Polish Jews were saved from extermination. Now, *that is* a legacy.

Or consider Rosa Parks, civil rights activist. Her courage inspired generations of freedom fighters to take up the cause of racial equality in the United States and abroad. Now, *that is* making a difference.

But who am I? I am just a simple working person. I have a job; I try to do my best; I pay my bills on time; I care for my family and friends. But that is about it. I am not changing the world and that is for sure, so what is this talk of leaving a legacy? Who am I kidding?

As a matter of fact, we are kidding ourselves if we think we are *not* leaving a legacy. Everything we do touches the lives of other people. All of our actions make a difference somehow. The way we live, the way we love, the work that we do, all have an effect that transcends the particulars of our day-to-day living. Whether we live a legacy life or not, the person we are stands as the difference we made when we die. It may be a small difference, but from the point of view of our own lives, it is *all* the difference there is. We cannot possibly underestimate the importance of our legacy because, in the end, it represents everything we were.

As Joseph Campbell put it so powerfully: "The call rings up the curtain, always, on the mystery of transfiguration.... The familiar life horizon has been outgrown; the old concepts, ideals, and emotional patterns no longer fit; the time for the passing of a threshold is at hand."

And this requires passing across a threshold into a deeper dimension of who we are. On a deeper, spiritual level this is what occurs when we reimagine our life's calling. When we find our voice, we can live a legacy life. By expressing our calling, we make our contribution, however large or small it may be, to our time.

Putting a Finish on Our Lives

James Hillman, in his book *The Force of Character*, makes the point that we often misunderstand the word "character." As it is used in the media and popular press, "character" tends to refer to only those aspects of our personality that are desirable. We talk, for example about how someone's character is defective or bad. But, as Hillman wants to emphasize, "character" originally simply referred to a person, regardless of who or what they were. Developing our character, therefore, is an activity of bringing forth *all* aspects of our personality, even those that we might be less than thrilled with. Hillman also talks about the "finish" of our lives in a way that distinguishes "finish" from "end." Finishing our lives, says Hillman is better understood as *putting a finish on* our lives—burnishing our character to a high gloss. This means making all aspects of our personality shine—even those less desirable ones. For instance, if we have a cantankerous and curmudgeonly character, we can burnish this by using it for social activism and change. Or, if our character is shy and retiring, we can burnish it by taking time for deep reflection on what really matters.

The point is, there is a natural connection between finishing our lives—putting a finish on our characters—and living the legacy we leave. Both require us to develop the most authentic expression of who we are. And there is no better starting point for this than our calling.

There is more to life than meets the eye—or any of the senses, for that matter. Heeding our life's calling requires a mode of searching that is not limited to the merely tangible. We need to connect with aspects of understanding that may be accessible only indirectly.

"Call Waiting"

When theologians talk about this, they sometimes refer to it as "listening with the third ear." The idea here is that our calling comes to us through uncharted pathways. Our two ears alone are not sensitive enough to pick up the subtle vibrations of calling.

Now this is not as far-fetched or "woo-woo" as it may at first sound. We have all had the experience of "just knowing" that something was right—or wrong—for us. Sometimes our ability to understand *that* a choice is best is greater than our ability to understand *why* it is. This does not mean we should never think carefully about things and reflect thoughtfully about the best courses of action; however, it does suggest that we also pay close attention to our intuitive side, our "third ear."

Assuming that messages about our calling can come to us indirectly, how can we prepare ourselves to receive them? How, in other words, can we train our "third ear" to listen more attentively?

One possibility is to become more sensitive to the signs of readiness to listen. Chief among these is a kind of restlessness in work, at home, and in our relationships with family members and friends. When we find ourselves continually "champing at the bit" for no obvious reason, it may be a sign that our calling is seeking expression. When the familiar begins to feel fatiguing and the usual unusually uninteresting, it is probably time for self-exploration to discover what is at the root of the problem. It is time to recognize that we probably have a "call waiting," and that it represents an opportunity to take our lives off hold.

Other signs of "call waiting" include a vague yearning for some different way of life, dreams of "chucking it all" and trying something completely different. Or we may find ourselves strangely obsessed with insignificant details; a hobby may take over our life unexpectedly. Procrastination, lack of energy, loss of focus, and just a general malaise are other indications that we are ready to answer the call in a new way.

What steps will enable us to do this? What actions permit us to make the connection we intuitively are seeking to make?

Courageous Conversations

In the movement toward expressing our calling, nothing is more powerful than honesty: honesty with friends, family members, and colleagues—but, above all, honesty with ourselves. We need to be willing to truthfully face up to the facts of our situations and if we are unhappy, to do something about it.

Having those "courageous conversations" with ourselves and others is never easy. But the alternative—living a life of regret—is ultimately, even harder.

We can begin by asking, "Is it worth it?" Are we willing to put up with the short-term pain of telling the truth to avoid the long-term dissatisfaction of a postponed life? Or is it simply too frightening to face the truth even though, in the long run, it will mean a greater chance of living a life of no regrets?

When it is put this way, most of us will probably agree that the former choice is preferable. It is easy to see that the long-term benefit justifies the short-term discomfort. It is worth wondering, therefore, why so many of us so typically opt for the latter. Is it just our inability to see the big picture?

If so, thinking about our legacy is one way we may be able to meet this challenge and inspire our courage. If we conceive of our lives with the end in mind, then what is truly important is easier to see. Taking the long-term perspective allows us to see how—in a relative way—the short-term pains pale in comparison to the long-term consequences of our choices. When we look back over our lives, we are able to recognize that the bumps in the road are just that—bumps. By comparison, what really makes a difference to the quality of the life that we have led is the road itself.

What Would I Do Differently?

We can explore the degree to which we are living a legacy life by reflecting upon our lives now as we might one day reflect upon them in the future. Pretend that Richard is interviewing you. He starts with this question: "If you could live your life over again, what would you do differently?"

Discuss your answers with a friend or family member. Examine together how you have lived—and how you might have lived differently.

Imagine that you are putting your answers together in a letter to a child, a grandchild, or someone you mentor. What will you say about how best to live? What insights can you share that will help them to reimagine their life's calling?

Take the time to actually write this letter. But substitute yourself—as you are right now—for future generations. What advice do you have from the person you are for the person you will be? How can that wisdom guide you as you reimagine your own life?

Remember the Charles Dickens classic *A Christmas Carol.* Recall the scene in which the Ghost of Christmas Future takes Scrooge to see his own. Even though the ghost emphasizes to Scrooge that what he is showing him is *not certain* to come to pass, the old miser is so affected by even the *prospect* of dying alone and unloved that he entirely changes his miserly ways overnight.

Of course, few of us face the sorts of regrets Scrooge was facing, but all of us have the potential for reimagining our lives in ways that will result in fewer regrets and a greater sense of purpose and meaning in the long run.

The "Reimagine Journey"

Virtually all cultures on earth have a story about a shared quest for meaning and transcendence—the "heroic" journey. Throughout the world's indigenous peoples, religions, and myths we find recognition of the journey toward legacy in human life. Our own individual legacies are a reminder that there is a vital spiritual dimension below the surface, a world of meaning that cannot be quantified, but must be lived.

When we think of our lives in this larger context, the core principles of calling reemerge with greater impact.

- **Calling comes from a caller.**

  Here we are reminded that each and every one of us is called and that turning our "third ear" to calling is a matter of turning to something larger than we are. Calling is heard inside, but it expresses itself outside. Becoming attuned to this inner voice from outside as we move through life's stages will enable us to craft a legacy of calling that is consistent with our deepest sense of why we are here.

- **Calling keeps calling.**

    Here we are reminded that calling is revealed to different people at different times in different ways. When we keep in mind the unique and individual nature of calling, we naturally recognize that we will express our calling in our own distinct ways during our lives. Our calling is unique to us but the manner in which we make calling manifest in the world is multifold. This realization can make us more apt to explore new ways to make our calling come alive. It can help us be more receptive to many alternatives for "playing our music."

- **Calling is personal.**

    Here we are reminded that there are as many callings in the world as there are people on the planet. If we live our entire life consistent with calling, we are likely to touch the lives of many other people. The opportunities for giving away our best-loved gifts to others will abound. Think of people you know who consistently express their calling through a lifetime of service to others. As we take a big picture perspective on our lives, we recognize even more clearly that what *really* matters is the chance to make a difference in the lives of others. With this big picture perspective we are better able to identify and take advantage of such opportunities when they appear.

- **Calling is connecting.**

    Uncovering our calling means making a deliberate choice to use our gifts to serve others and make a difference in the world. The legacy we leave is not created by a single act; rather, we will be remembered for the whole life we have led. And a life lived out of a connection to calling is far more likely to be remembered in the way we would like it to be. It is far more likely to matter in a way that matters to us. As long as we continue exploring our gifts, passions, and values—we reimagine the potential to add meaning in our lives—and the lives of those with whom we come in contact—each and every day of our lives.

Taking the broad perspective also reminds us that the ongoing inquiry into hearing and heeding our life's calling is not something that can be answered with simple checklists or standardized formulas. Callings are inherently mysterious; they tend to come to us in the form of questions rather than answers.

Perhaps in your own quest for calling, you can take some guidance from the stories of people in this book. If the voice of calling grows faint for you, you can reinforce it by recalling the voices of the people you have met here. They can reconnect you to that quiet place within from which the voice most important to you calls.

When you reconnect with that voice, listen to it. Let it help you uncover your calling. Let it inspire you to reimagine your work.

RESOURCES

Uncover your calling with Calling Cards™

The Work Reimagined Process works if you work the process! Reimagine your work by working the Calling Card process. What's your Calling Card? Take the free, online Calling Card assessment at lifereimagined.org.

- Do your own hands-on assessment using the Calling Cards kit from Inventure—The Purpose Company at richardleider.com.

- Do you want to continue the process of uncovering your calling? Visit the Life Reimagined online guidance process to explore new ways to reimagine your life and your work at lifereimagined.org.

- Subscribe to the free Life Reimagined email newsletter to receive new insight and regular updates at lifereimagined.org.

- Do you want to attend local live events or meet other Reimaginers in your community? Visit the Life Reimagined Community Events section at lifereimagined.org.

- Find out where Richard Leider may next be speaking at richardleider.com.

The Work Reimagined process continues!

INDEX

A

Acorn metaphor (seeds of destiny), 28–31
Acting on values, 118–119
Aristotle, 56–57, 66, 69, 102

B

Berry, Wendell, 65–66
Bidwell Training Center, 95–98
Boldt, Laurence, 65
Branding yourself, 9
Burnout, 49

C

Caller, defined, 15–16
Calling
    discovering, importance of, 1–3
    and economy of you, 8–9
    and finding fulling work, 22
    Guided Principles of, 13–17
    job-career-calling, 5–6
    and never working again, 6–8
    as opposed to job or career, 3–5
    as proactive summons, 37–38
    reimagining. *see* Calling, reimagining
    roots of, 26–27
    uncovering, 38–40
    uncovering our calling, 79–80
    Work 2.0, 10–11
Calling, reimagining
    death of purpose, 49–50
    gifts and good life, 56–60
    mattering matters, 61
    meaning and work, 46–48
    no getting out, 55–56
    no whiners allowed, 60–61
    perfect job, 45–46
    reimagining your job, 58–60
    relationship with money, 62–68
    risk of not reimagining, 48–49
    unlocking power of purpose, 50–55

151

What is success?, 68–70
working the process, 70–71
Calling Cards
    answering the Call, 87–89
    descriptor words, power of,
        81–83
    instructions for, 84–87
    list of, 83–84
    using, 80–81
Campbell, Joseph, 140
Carnegie Foundation, 95
Change, as new normal, 9
Checkup, Reimagined. *See* Work
    Reimagined Checkup
A Christmas Carol, 144–145
Connectedness and
    Contribution, 123–126
Connecting Self and Work, 37–38
Contingent workers, 8
Csikszentmihalyi, Mihaly, 75–76

D
Dalai Lama, 66, 125–126
Death of purpose, 49–50
Destiny, seeds of, 27–31
Dickens, Charles, 144–145

E
Economy of You, 8–9
Egg-drop game, 102–103
80/20 rule, 7
Emerson, Ralph Waldo, 93
Ethics for the New Millennium,
    125–126
Eudaimonia, 102

*Everything I Need to Know I
    Learned in Kindergarten*, 120

F
Faulkner, William, 94
*Flow: The Psychology of Optimal
    Experience*, 75–76
Frankl, Victor, 136
Fulghum, Robert, 120

G
Gifts, reimagining, 56–60
    calling as labor of love, 79–80
    expressing our gifts, 75–76
    napkin test, 73–74
    origins of gifts, 89–91
    passions, 76–78
    using calling cards, 80–89
    values, 78–79
    work, choosing or chosen, 74
Good life
    and gifts, 56–60
    and money, 63–64

H
Hand Dealt, 23–25, 89, 89–90,
    114
Happiness
    and money, 64–67
    as state of activity, 102
    and working, 6–8
Holmes, Oliver Wendell, 128
Huffington, Arianna, 69
Hurry Sickness, 48
Hutchings, Vicky, 103–104

I

"If you can't get out of it, get into it!", 54–55

Igniting Passion, 109–110

Immersion and passions, 102–105

Inner Kill, 49–50

Inner Urge, 130–131

Inventure, 51

J

Job, reimagining, 58–60

Job dissatisfaction, 121–123

Jobs, Steve, 75

Jobs

changes in over lifetime, 3–5, 8–9

Work 1.0, 9–10

K

Kahneman, Daniel, 64

Kant, Immanuel, 101

Karma, 90

Katselas, Tasso, 95

Kenya Outward Bound School, 51

L

Legacy, reimagining

defining our Inner Urge, 130–131

find your music, 129–130

Life Is Beautiful, 135–136

living a legacy life, 139–140

living your legacy, 131–133

playing your music, 127–129

putting the finish on life, 141

such is life, 134–135

What makes life beautiful?, 136–138

What would I do differently, 144–145

wisdom: #1 regret, 138–139

Life

living your legacy, 139–140

as proactive summons, 94–98

putting the finish on, 141

What would I do differently, 144–145

Life Is Beautiful, 135–136

Logotherapy, 136

M

Manchester Craftsmen's Guild (MCG), 95–98

Mattering, importance of, 61

Meaning and Work, 46–48

The Meaning of Life, 93

Michener, James, 93

Mill, John Stuart, 101

Money, relationship with

and the good life, 63–64

and happiness, 64–67

how much is enough?, 62–63

where is it going?, 119–121

Moorhead, Hugh S., 93

Mr. Holland's Opus, 128

Music

find yours, 129–130

playing yours, 127–129

N

Napkin Test, 73–74

"nature vs. nurture", 89

New York Times, 4

The Nichomachean Ethics, 56

Novachis, John, 6–8

#1 Regret, 138–139

O

One-Year Test, 98–100

P

Parents, as role models, 34–35

Parks, Rosa, 140

Passions, reimagining
  absorbed and immersed,
    102–105
  igniting, 109–110
  life as possibilities, 94–98
  making work work, 100–102
  and meaning of life, 93–94
  One-Year Test, 98–100
  passions as gifts, 76–78
  in work, 105–109

Perfect job, 45–46

Personal story, changing, 40–43

Pilgrim Center for Reconciliation,
  106

Plato, 102

Preferences, 84–86

Principles of Calling
  1. Calling Comes from Caller,
    15–16, 146
  2. Calling Keeps Calling, 16,
    146

  3. Calling Is Personal, 16–17,
    146
  4. Calling Is Connection, 17,
    146–147

Pritchard, Derek, 51–55

Process of reimagining, 70–71

Purpose, death of, 49–50

Purpose, unlocking, 50–55

Q

Questions for reimagining work
  What do you do?, 21–22
  What do you want to be
    when you grow up?,
    22–26

R

Radhakrishnan, Sarvepalli, 90

Reimagine Journey
  Calling Comes from a Caller,
    143
  Calling Is Connecting,
    146–147
  Calling Is Personal, 146
  Calling Keeps Calling, 146

Reimagining Calling. *See*
  Calling, reimagining

Reimagining Gifts. *See* Gifts,
  reimagining

Reimagining Legacy. *See* Legacy,
  reimagining

Reimagining Passions. *See*
  Passions, reimagining

Reimagining Work. *See* Work,
  reimagining

Repacking Your Bags, 42

Role Models, 34–37
Roosevelt, Theodore, 93
Ross, Frank, 97
Rouner, Arthur, 106–109
Rouner, Molly, 106–109

S

Schindler, Arthur, 139
Slash career, 4
Solving for Pattern, 65–66
Story, personal, 40–43
Strickland, Bill, 94–100, 104
Success, 68–70
"Such Is Life," 134–135

T

Telos, 102
Thrive, 69
Time magazine, 107

V

Values, reimagining
    acting on values, 118–119
    connectedness and
        contribution, 123–126
    as deepest beliefs, as gifts,
        78–79
    hand life has dealt, 114–115
    money, spending, 119–121
    no perfect jobs, 121–123
    only a job, 110–113
    valuing our values, 115–118
Vocation, defined, 37
Voyageur Outward Bound
    School, 51

W

Website, Life Reimagined, 83
Whiners not allowed, 60–61
Wisdom of the Ages, 138–139
Words, power of, 81–83
Work, choosing or chosen, 74
Work, making it work, 100–102
Work, reimagining
    changes in work style, 8–13
    changing stories to self,
        40–43
    connecting self and work,
        37–38
    destiny, seeds of, 27–31
    role models, 34–37
    uncovering our calling,
        38–40
    What do you do?, 21–22
    What do you want to be
        when you grow up?,
        22–26
    what you love, not what you
        should, 31–34
Work 1.0, 9–10
Work 2.0, 10–11
Work and Meaning, 46–48
Work Reimagined Checkup, 18,
    46, 47–48

Z

*Zen and the Art of Making a
    Living*, 65

ABOUT THE AUTHORS

Richard J. Leider

Richard Leider, founder of Inventure—the Purpose Company, is ranked by *Forbes Magazine* as one of the "Top 5" most respected executive coaches in America and by The Conference Board as a "legend in coaching."

Richard's nine books have sold over one million copies and have been translated into twenty languages. The best sellers *Repacking Your Bags* and *The Power of Purpose* are considered classics in the personal development field.

As coauthor of *Life Reimagined,* Richard is the Chief Curator of content for AARP's *Life Reimagined Institute.* Widely viewed as a visionary and thought leader on the "power of purpose," he is featured regularly in many media sources including Public Broadcasting Service (PBS) and National Public Radio (NPR).

Richard holds a master's degree in Counseling and is a National Certified Career Counselor and a National Certified Master Career Counselor. As a Senior Fellow at the University of Minnesota's Center for Spirituality and Healing, he founded the Purpose Project, an ongoing initiative to explore the power of purpose in life and work. He is a Carlson Executive Fellow at the University of Minnesota School of Management and cochairman of the Linkage/Global Institute for Leadership Development.

He is a contributing author to many coaching books, including *Coaching for Leadership, The Art and Practice of Leadership Coaching, Executive Coaching for Results,* and *The Organization of the Future.*

Richard's work has been recognized with awards from the Bush Foundation, from which he was awarded a Bush Fellowship, and the Fielding Institute, which awarded him their Outstanding Scholar for Creative Longevity and Wisdom Award. He was named a "Distinguished Alumnus" by Gustavus Adolphus College, and was named to the "Hall of Fame" at Central High School in St. Paul, Minnesota.

For thirty years, Richard has led Inventure Expedition walking safaris in Tanzania, East Africa, where he cofounded and is a board member of the Dorobo Fund for Tanzania.

Richard and his wife, Sally, live on the St. Croix River outside Minneapolis, Minnesota.

ABOUT THE AUTHORS

David A. Shapiro

David A. Shapiro is a writer, philosopher, and educator who specializes in exploring questions about ethics and the good life.

A full-time faculty member at Cascadia College, a two-year comprehensive community college near Seattle, Washington, David is also Education Director of the University of Washington Center for Philosophy for Children, a nonprofit organization that brings philosophy and philosophers into the lives of young people in schools and community forums.

David is the author of *Choosing the Right Thing to Do: In Life, At Work, In Relationships, and For the Planet,* and *Plato Was Wrong! Footnotes on Doing Philosophy with Young People*, and coauthor with Richard Leider of five books, including the best-seller, *Repacking Your Bags: Lighten Your Load for the Good Life.*

David is a longtime student and practitioner of Ashtanga Yoga in the tradition of Sri K. Pattabhi Jois, and an avid cycling commuter.

He lives in Seattle, Washington, with his wife, Jennifer Dixon, and daughter, Mimi Dixon-Shapiro.

Also by Richard J. Leider, with Alan M. Webber

Life Reimagined
Discovering Your New Life Possibilities

Are you at a point in your life where you're asking, "What's next?" You've finished one chapter and you have yet to write the next one. Here is your map to guide you in this new life phase. You can use the powerful practices and insights—enhanced with online tools and exercises at AARP's LifeReimagined.org website—to help you uncover your own special gifts, connect with people who can support you, and explore new directions.

You'll be inspired by meeting ordinary people who have reimagined their lives in extraordinary ways. You'll also read the stories of pioneers of the Life Reimagined movement, such as Jane Pauley, James Brown, and Emilio Estefan. They show us that this journey of discovery can help us find fulfillment in surprising new places. Let *Life Reimagined* help you discover your new life possibilities!

Paperback, 192 pages, ISBN 978-1-60994-932-7
PDF ebook ISBN 978-1-60994-953-2

BK° Berrett–Koehler Publishers, Inc.
www.bkconnection.com   **800.929.2929**

Berrett–Koehler
Publishers

Berrett-Koehler is an independent publisher dedicated to an ambitious mission: *Creating a World That Works for All.*

We believe that to truly create a better world, action is needed at all levels—individual, organizational, and societal. At the individual level, our publications help people align their lives with their values and with their aspirations for a better world. At the organizational level, our publications promote progressive leadership and management practices, socially responsible approaches to business, and humane and effective organizations. At the societal level, our publications advance social and economic justice, shared prosperity, sustainability, and new solutions to national and global issues.

A major theme of our publications is "Opening Up New Space." Berrett-Koehler titles challenge conventional thinking, introduce new ideas, and foster positive change. Their common quest is changing the underlying beliefs, mindsets, institutions, and structures that keep generating the same cycles of problems, no matter who our leaders are or what improvement programs we adopt.

We strive to practice what we preach—to operate our publishing company in line with the ideas in our books. At the core of our approach is stewardship, which we define as a deep sense of responsibility to administer the company for the benefit of all of our "stakeholder" groups: authors, customers, employees, investors, service providers, and the communities and environment around us.

We are grateful to the thousands of readers, authors, and other friends of the company who consider themselves to be part of the "BK Community." We hope that you, too, will join us in our mission.

A BK Life Book

This book is part of our BK Life series. BK Life books change people's lives. They help individuals improve their lives in ways that are beneficial for the families, organizations, communities, nations, and world in which they live and work. To find out more, visit **www.bk-life.com**.

Berrett–Koehler
Publishers

A community dedicated to creating
a world that works for all

Dear Reader,

Thank you for picking up this book and joining our worldwide community of Berrett-Koehler readers. We share ideas that bring positive change into people's lives, organizations, and society.

To welcome you, we'd like to offer you a free ebook. You can pick from among twelve of our bestselling books by entering the promotional code **BKP92E** here: http://www.bkconnection.com/welcome.

When you claim your free ebook, we'll also send you a copy of our e-newsletter, the *BK Communiqué*. Although you're free to unsubscribe, there are many benefits to sticking around. In every issue of our newsletter you'll find

- A free ebook
- Tips from famous authors
- Discounts on spotlight titles
- Hilarious insider publishing news
- A chance to win a prize for answering a riddle

Best of all, our readers tell us, "Your newsletter is the only one I actually read." So claim your gift today, and please stay in touch!

Sincerely,

Charlotte Ashlock
Steward of the BK Website

Questions? Comments? Contact me at bkcommunity@bkpub.com.